DISARMING EUROPE

DISARMING EUROPE

Edited by

Mary Kaldor
and
Dan Smith

THE MERLIN PRESS
LONDON

© The Merlin Press 1982

This edition first published by
The Merlin Press
3 Manchester Road
London E14

printed by Whitstable Litho Ltd
Whitstable Kent

typesetting by Heather Hems
The Malt House, Chilmark, Wilts.

Cover design by Louis Mackay

British Library Cataloguing in Publication Data

Disarming Europe.
  1. Peace — Societies, etc — History
  2. Europe — Politics and government — History
  I. Kaldor, Mary   II. Smith, Dan
  327.1'72'094   JX1952

ISBN 0-85036-277-6
ISBN 0-85036-278-4 Pbk

CONTENTS

Introduction   ix
    Mary Kaldor and Dan Smith

Part I: Arming Europe

Nuclear Strategy and Technology   3
    Allan Krass and Dan Smith

Nuclear Weapons in Europe   35
    William Arkin

Theatre Nuclear Weapons: The NATO Doctrine   65
    Sverre Lodgaard

Theatre Nuclear Weapons: The Soviet Doctrine   89
    David Holloway

The Role of Nuclear Weapons in Western Relations   105
    Mary Kaldor

Part II: Disarming Europe

Nuclear Weapons and East-West Relations: A
Socialist View   127
    István Kende

For a Nordic Nuclear-Weapon-Free Zone   135
    Erik Alfsen

Western European Neutralism   143
    Ulrich Albrecht

Alternative Defence Policies and Modern Weapon
Technology   163
    Ben Dankbaar

Nuclear Disarmament: Non-Nuclear Defence   185
    Anders Boserup

Glossary   193

Notes on Authors   195

ACKNOWLEDGEMENT

The END Research Conference in Amsterdam in May 1981 on which this book is based was made possible by financial support from END, CND and the Transnational Institute. The editors are extremely grateful for this assistance.

INTRODUCTION

Mary Kaldor and Dan Smith

The Appeal for European Nuclear Disarmament was launched at the end of April 1980. Since then it has been widely canvassed throughout Europe, both East and West, and in the USA, and has received an astonishing range of support.

The Appeal's basic themes are straightforward. It argues that the danger of nuclear war occurring is on the increase as already massive nuclear arsenals grow and as doctrines are developed which attempt to emphasise the utility of nuclear weapons. As a major step towards disarmament and a secure peace, the Appeal calls upon the people of Europe to act together to free our continent of nuclear weapons. For this, a massive popular movement is required, with different strategies in each country suited to particular national conditions, but working for the common goal.

Straightforward as these themes are, they raise a host of issues which have to be examined further so that the disarmament movements can understand more clearly both where we are (and how we got here) as well as where we should go (and how to get there). To contribute to this, we convened a conference of researchers in Amsterdam at the end of May 1981 to discuss European nuclear disarmament. But the participants were not purely academics, and our discussions were not purely academic. In different ways, the participants were all active in disarmament movements in their own countries, and thus brought to the conference a scholarly concern to clarify the issues, together with a political concern to develop a strategy for disarmament.

This book contains the papers discussed at the conference, together with others written since then. Our introduction sets out some of the concerns which unify the different strands pursued in the various contributions, and highlights aspects of the discussion not fully encompassed in the rest of the book.

The demand for a nuclear-free Europe is impelled, first and foremost, by fear of nuclear war. Part I of the book, 'Arming Europe', explores the dimensions of the situation which creates this fear—the weapons, strategies and politics of the new Cold War. It is perhaps ironic that these essays are both longer and more complex than those which make up Part II, 'Disarming Europe'. But we do not apologise for this. The current situation is alarmingly dangerous, but also highly complex. It is part of the task of peace researchers to explain as fully as is necessary the elements of this situation.

In Chapter 1, Allan Krass and Dan Smith provide an overview of strategic and technological developments in the superpower nuclear arms race that forms the backdrop to any consideration of the European situation. Perhaps even more alarming than the sheer quantitative increase in nuclear warheads over the past two decades has been the shift in strategy away from pure deterrence as most people still seem to understand it—a matter of preparing a single massive retaliatory strike to nuclear aggression—towards more 'flexible' notions about the use of nuclear weapons. Krass and Smith argue that this shift is an inevitable consequence of the weaknesses of pure deterrence. Nuclear deterrence involves an implicit willingness to commit national suicide and puts both political and military leaders into difficult positions. So both are constantly seeking ways in which deterrence can be made more 'credible'. They seek a political and strategic utility in nuclear weapons. At the same time technological development increases the accuracy of nuclear weapons, seeming to open up new possibilities for nuclear weapons to be useable. But Krass and Smith also show that the new strategies involve even greater risks than the old. The apparently hard-headed logic of these strategies almost wilfully ignores the dangers they are creating and the logical contradictions they are built on. Flirting with ideas of 'limited' nuclear war, and deploying forces which fit such concepts, is increasing the risk of the nuclear holocaust.

Chapter 2 by Bill Arkin describes the nuclear weapons designed for theatre nuclear war in Europe. In the 1970s both NATO and the Warsaw Pact brought in new theatre nuclear forces. For the 1980s, both sides are planning further additions: cruise missiles and Pershing IIs for NATO, along with an extensive modernisation programme for battlefield nuclear weapons (including the so-called 'neutron' bomb); on the Warsaw Pact side, continuing deployment of the SS-20 Intermediate Range Ballistic Missile and SS-21 short-range missile is likely to be supplemented by the SS-22 and SS-X-23 Medium Range Ballistic Missiles. Arkin argues that nuclear weapons are so closely integrated into the equipment and planning of combat units in Europe that it is impossible to conceive of violent conflict in Europe in which nuclear weapons remain unused.

Chapters 3 and 4 by Sverre Lodgaard and David Holloway respectively consider the doctrines under which these nuclear forces are deployed. Looking at NATO strategy, Lodgaard examines the contradictory and controversial arguments about whether the introduction of cruise and Pershing II ties the defence of Western Europe more or less closely to the defence of the USA. He shows that even among the proponents of these new deployments there are irreconcilable differences of view, and that the new weapons do not solve the problems they are thought to by the proponents. Soviet theatre nuclear strategy is ill understood in the West; Holloway describes its development and its main components. In particular, he looks at how shifts in Western strategy have affected Soviet doctrines for theatre nuclear forces. Just as every new weapon system on one side is countered by the other, so every new strategy draws forth a counter-strategy.

Increases in weaponry and strategic shifts occur within the context of the new Cold War. In part, this can be traced to the American response to the realities of relative US decline in the 1970s. This weakening of US leadership of the advanced capitalist countries has been caused by numerous interlocking factors. Undoubtedly, the USA's defeat in Vietnam has played a part, as did the traumas of 'Watergate'; James Carter's Presidency was marked by continual vacillations in major policy. But the root of the problem is the USA's relative economic decline, with growth rates and productivity in Japan and Western Europe outpacing the USA's. Caspar Weinberger, the US Defense Secretary, has characterised the Reagan administration as having a two-part programme 'to revitalize America'. The first half is economic, based on policies and theories known in the USA as 'supply-side economics' and in Britain as 'monetarism'. The second half is 'the revitalization of American military strength'.[1] The theme is that strength must replace weakness. Political logic dictates that this be reflected in language as well as policy, and that in turning away from the era of weakness the USA should turn its back on everything associated with that era including, most notably, detente and the 1979 Strategic Arms Limitation agreement (SALT II) with the USSR.

In Chapter 5 Mary Kaldor discusses the way in which this renewed emphasis on leadership is linked to thinking on nuclear weapons. Nuclear weapons have always been a unifying element in NATO, embodying and emphasising US leadership around which the other states can cohere. Today, there is no issue more divisive within the alliance than nuclear weapons. As Sverre Lodgaard's chapter also brings out, there is a fundamental incompatibility between how the USA views nuclear strategy and the ways in which the European members of NATO have viewed it. For the latter, nuclear strategy has basically been about ensuring they are protected by US nuclear deterrence. There have always been problems about the credibility of this protection—the nagging question, Would the President risk Chicago to save Dusseldorf? US interest in strategic concepts which emphasise the war-fighting function and limited use of nuclear weapons is precisely an effort to avoid risking Chicago. Thus, what the Western European states want and seem to think they are getting from the US 'nuclear umbrella' is not what the USA is actually offering. And while the Western European states try desperately to convince themselves and the rest of us that the American umbrella is what they say it is, abundant evidence exists in the USA to show that it is really something quite different and far less comforting.

So the old orthodoxies are no longer so sturdy. Tensions between Western Europe and the USA will not only be expressed in the odd language of nuclear strategy, but over economic policies and political relations with other countries. In the midst of profound economic and political crisis, the Atlanticist consensus shows signs of strain and more. All this cannot be wished away, eradicated by firm words on the American side of the Atlantic and soothing words on the European side. The depth of the problem is not surprising: what is at stake in the current crisis is the durability of an international economic and political order established in the wake of World War II. The cement of that order has been American power. One of the binding constituents has been American nuclear capability. Most Western European defence policies have been predicated on that capability for thirty years. Dependence on that capability has entailed and symbolised acceptance of US leadership. Breaking that nuclear tie has always been unthinkable, yet accepting it and strengthening it has become deeply problematic. Atlanticism is looking for a way to turn.

In the USSR, foreign policy has not undergone any abrupt discontinuity. But in a variety of ways, Soviet actions have contributed to a mutual process with the USA which have eroded the spirit of detente. The Soviet arms build-up, though consistently exaggerated in the Western press, has been unremitting. Relevant or not, continued domestic repression in the USSR eroded public support for detente in the West. In 1978 in particular, the USA and USSR got involved in a series of niggling diplomatic actions against each other. Soviet adventures in Angola and Ethiopia and its general search for greater influence in Third World politics appeared to threaten the American position. The invasion of Afghanistan at the end of 1979 indicated a willingness for the first time in years to risk Soviet soldiers in sustained combat outside the Warsaw Pact area of Eastern Europe. This readiness to participate directly in armed conflict may mark a change in Soviet attitudes about the use of armed force, about which they have previously been much more cautious than the USA.

At the Amsterdam conference, Vittorio Orilia, a foreign affairs spokesperson of the Italian Communist Party, reported on his impressions from a recent visit to several Eastern European countries. Owing to his tragic death shortly after the conference, we are unable to include a written version of his remarks as a chapter of this book. Our own summary of his remarks cannot do justice to them.

Orilia argued that the rigidification of Eastern Europe cannot last. The developments in Poland are well known, but tensions and difficulties simmer also in Hungary and East Germany. Both countries have a lot to lose from a new Cold War. Both have managed to achieve a reasonable standard of living, and Hungarians enjoy a measure of democracy, apparent in more open discussion and more public criticism than is possible in the other countries. These gains can only be consolidated through increased economic and cultural contacts with the West, which become increasingly difficult with the return to Cold War. The political process which might loosen the rigidity is likely to be different in each Eastern European country. Orilia anticipated that if there were to be greater degrees of autonomy from the USSR, this would more probably be achieved through political shifts within the ruling Communist Parties, rather than through the development of new mass political forces as in Poland.

The nature of the Soviet response is obviously a crucial element. The military clamp-down in Poland in December 1981 showed the limits to independent political development in Eastern Europe. Yet in the year before the clamp-down, there was evidence of real uncertainty within the Soviet leadership, of a division between those who favoured an essentially hard-line response, and those who preferred an accommodation of at least some aspects of the reformist drive. The Polish clamp-down cannot entirely remove the pressure for reform, either in Poland or elsewhere in Eastern Europe, but in its wake it has become apparent that military confrontation and renewed Cold War provide the least favourable context for change. Detente and disarmament may therefore be the only route to political change and greater autonomy for Eastern European countries.

Deepened military confrontation and restrengthened repression will impose real economic and political costs on the USSR. This is why there are those, even after December 1981, who would prefer to accommodate some aspects of reformism. Yet this may be feared as a beginning to a gradual process which will eventually unravel the post-1945 order in Eastern Europe. Accommodating reformism in Eastern Europe may also mean encouraging reformism in the USSR itself. To some extent, these dilemmas mirror those of American policy, in which the confrontation politics of Weinberger are balanced against the more sensitive Atlanticism attributed to Haig.

The future in Europe will be critically shaped by what happens in the East, by further political developments there and by the Soviet response. Developments in US policy and NATO's internal politics will be similarly important. And these two decisive sets of issues are closely connected, for the hardliners in one superpower provide the justification for the hardliners in the other. If the hardliners on either side manage to get a lasting grip on policy, the result could be to set in motion a conflict of wills that could end in war— nuclear war. Only if a certain degree of autonomy of the Western and Eastern European states from their respective superpowers can be established will there be an opportunity for a real alternative to war, for genuine measures of disarmament. And vice versa—in other words, independent political development in Europe and disarmament must proceed together. This is the basic task in a strategy for European nuclear disarmament.

The Appeal for European Nuclear Disarmament stated that:

> We must act together to free the entire territory of Europe, from Poland to Portugal, from nuclear weapons, air and submarine bases, and from all institutions engaged in research into or manufacture of nuclear weapons.[2]

As Ken Coates has put it, the 'Poland to Portugal' formulation

does not imply an unwillingness to negotiate the denuclearization of

European Russia right up to the Urals: it merely registers the existing real division between the superpowers, East and West, on the one side, and the states of Europe, which are caught up in the effects of the arms race between those powers, like corks bobbing on the flood, on the other.[3]

But while the *politics* of the formulation may be right, the discussion of the END objective in terms of creating a European nuclear-free zone (NFZ) does raise the question of the zone's geographical boundaries. The discussion of this question at the Amsterdam conference resulted in a position which does not so much *solve* the problem as *displace* it.

NFZs are a standard part of the 'armoury' of proposals for arms control and disarmament. They were, for example, endorsed in the Final Statement of the United Nations Special Session on Disarmament in 1978; the Treaty of Tlatelolco provides an example of an effort to put the proposal into practice, by making Latin America into a NFZ. But there is a wide variety of disarmament proposals, which can be classified in two ways.

First, it is necessary to distinguish between proposals which focus on certain *categories of weapons* (as in the disarmament movements' demands—no cruise, no Pershing II, no SS-20) and those which aim for the reduction or elimination of *nuclear weapons in a given area*—NFZs, or 'security zones' in which nuclear weapons would be reduced to the lowest level possible.

Second, it is necessary to distinguish between proposals for *multilateral action* by two or more states after negotiation, and proposals for *unilateral action* by individual states without negotiating with adversaries.

In the discussion at Amsterdam it was generally agreed that *all four* approaches need to be followed: single-minded concentration on particular types or categories of weapons could lead to a hollow victory. Even if the disarmament movements succeed in preventing the deployment of cruise and Pershing II missiles, the American forward-based systems, the British and French systems and battlefield nuclear weapons will all remain. The campaign for a European NFZ provides a vehicle for bringing into focus the entire range of nuclear weapons in Europe.

At the same time, exclusive emphasis on NFZs could simply result in a geographical shift in the danger of war—SS-20s deployed east of the Urals, but still capable of striking Western Europe; cruise missiles deployed on submarines.

The disadvantages of multilateral approaches to disarmament have been widely discussed in the disarmament movements. Twenty years of multilateral negotiations have not prevented the spiralling arms race. At most, they have prevented the further development of anti-ballistic missiles (though interest in these weapons is now reviving) and have achieved the dismantling of stockpiles of bacteriological weapons. The negotiations have effectively legitimised the continued arms race and provided new rationales for armament. One of the main justifications for cruise and Pershing II, after all, is as a bargaining chip to be set against the SS-20 in negotiations with the USSR. The only way out of the multilateral deadlock is through independent action, through the refusal of governments to continue participating in this madness.

Yet it is also likely that, were a disarmament process to begin through unilateral action, it would still be necessary and perhaps at last possible to confirm and even achieve disarmament measures through multilateral agreement. Indeed, unilateral action could almost be viewed as a kind of negotiation, but one made outside the usual diplomatic forums.

To return to the proposal of a European NFZ, it is clear that it has the advantage of focusing attention on the full range of the nuclear threat to Europe. But its disadvantage, at least potentially, is that it may seem to wrap up an extremely complex process in a single negotiating package. It implies a single act of disarmament—one set of negotiations towards one treaty—when it should be obvious that European nuclear disarmament is going to be an immensely complex task. Reliance on nuclear weapons is deeply embedded in the politico-military establishments of Europe; digging them out will be long and difficult work. Progress towards the ultimate objective will be made in different ways and at different speeds in different countries. In this context, it could well be counter-productive if NATO and the Warsaw Pact sat down tomorrow to negotiate a European NFZ, because they would sit there for so long. It is therefore necessary both to think of partial steps towards the objective of a nuclear-free Europe, and to propose unilateral actions to break the multilateralist deadlock. The task of END is a political task, to be achieved in the political arena—not a diplomatic task for a diplomatic arena.

In the end, the final steps towards a European NFZ might be taken on the basis of negotiation and agreement. Certainly, a treaty declaring Europe to be a NFZ would be a useful way of codifying the situation. But there is a multiplicity of routes for arriving at that point, and the idea of a NFZ treaty should not be allowed to distract attention from the immediate objectives of taking the first steps along that road.

Part II of this book, 'Disarming Europe', provides a discussion of some of this multiplicity of routes to European nuclear disarmament. It is, however, only a partial discussion. In Chapter 6 István Kende sets out the various multilateral options that could be pursued from the Warsaw Pact point of view. In Chapter 7, Erik Alfsen presents the arguments for and against a Nordic NFZ as a partial step towards a European NFZ, and describes what such an agreement could include.

The Nordic NFZ would not only be a way of codifying the existing situation in that part of Europe, as a way of preventing any build-up of nuclear weapons in that region, it could also be a way in which non-nuclear states can put pressure on the superpowers—on the USSR to remove nuclear weapons from the Kola Peninsula, and on the USA to desist from a nuclear build-up in and around the Nordic area. It was pointed out at Amsterdam that a possible disadvantage of a Nordic NFZ would be to eliminate any positive influence from non-nuclear Denmark and Norway over NATO's nuclear strategy. In the controversy over the deployment of cruise and Pershing II missiles, neither Denmark nor Norway has supported the position of the Dutch government, assuming instead a rather passive and quiescent role. This is why the Norwegian disarmament movement puts so much emphasis on combining the campaign for a Nordic NFZ with the campaign against cruise and Pershing II. The point is to move the Norwegian government into a position where it confirms Norway's non-nuclear status, codifies Scandinavia's non-nuclear status, and seeks wider measures of nuclear disarmament in Europe.

Alfsen's analysis provides an excellent basis for considering proposals in other regions. The Nordic NFZ, copied and extended elsewhere in Europe, would not be as important for what it might achieve in time of war as for what it might achieve in time of peace, to prevent that war ever occurring.

At the Amsterdam conference, there was a great deal of discussion of NFZs and security zones. In Chapter 8, Ulrich Albrecht explores the political implications, as well as the history, of such proposals for central Europe, examining different options for disengagement right at the fulcrum of East-West confrontation. Albrecht's essay is essentially an effort to indicate the long-considered possibilities of some other kind of approach to East-West relations besides confrontation. A different approach could well be part of the basis for at least eroding the barrier between East and West in Europe, for breaking down the Cold War division of the continent. There is clearly a need to extend this discussion, considering also the role of security zones in, for example, the Mediterranean region.

Disarmament needs to be seen not simply as a negative—the opposite of armament, the rejection of current policies. It must also be seen as positive action, seeking alternative and more effective solutions to the problem of security in the widest sense, including both economic and political aspects. Sweden provides an example of a country which, having opted both for non-alignment and for a non-nuclear position, has been able to campaign for action on disarmament in the international political and diplomatic arena. This could be seen as a way of approaching a strengthening of multilateral approaches to disarmament by beginning with unilateral action.

A further perspective on this is provided by Chapters 9 and 10, by Ben Dankbaar and Anders Boserup respectively. They consider the possibilities of alternative and non-nuclear defence policies. In this perspective, unilateral nuclear disarmament is carried out, not as a gesture, but as a shift in defence policy which could begin to change the military equation in Europe. Dankbaar's chapter reviews various approaches to conventional defence in a nuclear age made by military experts in Europe. Boserup explains the fundamental flaws of nuclear deterrence, but argues that raising the 'nuclear threshold' in Europe cannot be achieved merely by strengthening existing conventional forces. Instead, taking up themes in the literature reviewed by Dankbaar, he argues for a fundamental shift in force planning, deliberately weakening offensive forces, while increasing defensive strength. While weapon systems themselves may be used in both offensive and defensive modes, Boserup argues that force structures and deployments as a whole can clearly reveal a concentration on offence or defence. If Western European states moved towards a concentration on defensive forces, this could make NATO nuclear weapons unnecessary, and render those of the Warsaw Pact inoperable. It is possible that these two chapters are the most important in this book, revealing in general terms ways forward for defence policy which do not involve the threat of nuclear suicide, and emphasising the need to translate this approach into specific policies for each country.

In order to achieve the reduction and ultimately the elimination of nuclear arsenals in Europe, there will have to be a solid and durable political basis for disarmament. What has been happening in Western Europe since the December 1979 decision by NATO to deploy cruise and Pershing II missiles is the development of this political basis.

During that time, the disarmament movements have focused on specific and immediate demands which reject the further steps in the arms race of new 'theatre' nuclear missiles, of the neutron bomb and of Trident. As they have developed, the movements have begun to draw attention to the full panoply of preparations for nuclear war in Europe. And they have understood from the beginning that it is necessary to exert what pressure is possible on the USSR to reduce its forces for nuclear war in Europe.

In doing this, a quite remarkable and unique coalition has begun to emerge. Those who decry the disarmament movements of Western Europe as left-wing movements (or those who applaud them as such) have simply failed to understand the nature of that coalition. The breadth of concern is quite astonishing. Not only the Eurocommunist and Euro-socialist parties have been drawn into the movement, but also forces in the centre of the political spectrum and some towards the right. In Holland and also in West Germany, the churches have been a central part of the movement. In north-western Europe as a whole, the independent disarmament movements are alliances which go through and around the main political parties, bringing into political activity many who have no experience of party-political activism at all. In southern Europe, one would normally expect there to be less political 'space' for mass movements independent of the main parties. Yet in Italy, it appears that a strong and flourishing network of local disarmament groups is emerging into an autonomous disarmament movement. In Norway, the atmosphere of resisting the nuclear threat has been likened to that of the resistance to Nazi rule in World War II—the same urgency, the same determination, the same unity transcending other political differences.

Yet movements in different parts of Europe, with different political traditions and cultures, should not be expected all to look alike. Nor will they necessarily share exactly the same approaches, either to issues of policy or to methods of campaigning. They work in different political contexts which create different kinds of possibilities and impose different kinds of constraints upon them. The issues are not the same in each country.

Despite these differences, the coalition which is emerging is not only politically broad, but also crosses national boundaries. Increasingly it is understood both that there can be no single coordinating centre for the European disarmament movements—that they cannot be forged into a single movement—and that it is nonetheless necessary for there to be a measure of coordination in both their politics and their strategies.

A prime example of this need is offered by the issue of the negotiations on long-range theatre nuclear forces begun in Geneva between the USA and USSR on 30 November 1981.

It is clear that the USA entered these talks in part because of the need to do something to quieten the anxieties of Western European public opinion, as evidenced in massive demonstrations during October and November 1981. The participants at the Amsterdam conference generally agreed that these negotiations could be supported if they were about real reductions in the nuclear forces of both sides. If they became another cosmetic exercise, actually permitting increases on both sides, they could only be attacked as a sham. It was also agreed that whether or not the negotiations took place, the disarmament movements must not stop pressing their governments to withdraw their consent to the NATO decision to deploy cruise and Pershing II missiles. At the same time, the USSR should be pressed to reduce or eliminate its SS-20s. This position was later expressed in the Hiroshima Day Appeal issued jointly by END and the Dutch Inter-Church Peace Council.

The lead-up to the Geneva talks showed how necessary this vigilance is. President Reagan offered American cancellation of the cruise and Pershing II deployments (thus also revealing the extent to which the USA can speak for the whole of NATO), as long as the USSR dismantled its older SS-4 and SS-5 missiles along with its SS-20s. Thus, *existing* NATO theatre nuclear forces would be untouched: a unilateral reduction (by the USSR), but bilaterally agreed—a revolutionary concept of disarmament. One may speculate about the Western reaction if President Brezhnev offered not to deploy, say, SS-30s in exchange for the USA removing all nuclear capable aircraft from Europe and from aircraft carriers around Europe.

In November 1981, it was clear that the USA and, to judge by their reactions to the Reagan proposal, the Western European governments wanted the disarmament movements to go away. It did not appear that they were willing to negotiate actual disarmament in order to achieve this. It was also clear that the Reagan proposal was exactly the same as the original 'dual track decision'—to deploy cruise and Pershing II missiles and to seek arms control talks about SS-20s. The disarmament movements have been built on the basis of opposition to that decision. There was no need for them to change their minds despite the propaganda barrage in the Western European press. Yet the risk that some of the movements might be weakened by this development, that some components of the coalitions would drift away believing that NATO was now persuaded of the need for disarmament, was high. The greatest clarity on the issues and maximum communication between the movements are the preconditions for insisting that real disarmament take place.

As the disarmament movements develop further, the arguments will move from an analysis and rejection of the risks of the current situation towards definite strategies and policies for the future. Here, as we have already said, further and more specific study of the issues raised in Chapters 9 and 10 of this book will be crucial. But these will themselves be shaped by the attitudes which are taken about the nature of the Western European relationship to the superpowers. At the moment, as junior partners, we are all too obviously included in superpower confrontation. Nuclear weapons based in Europe and the basing of Western European defence policies on US nuclear capabilities have been major ways of tying Western Europe into the American alliance. Thus, any proposal for a genuine reduction of nuclear forces in Europe, even if the reductions are even-handed between American and Soviet weapons, is bound to untie Western Europe, at least partially, from the Atlantic alliance. At the same time, the Appeal for European Nuclear Disarmament calls upon Europeans to learn to be loyal, not to 'East' and 'West', but to each other. It seeks a loosening of the Cold War bonds on Eastern Europe as well, and proposes to approach this via a reduction in armaments and the tense politics of confrontation.

This does not mean ignoring the East-West division and confrontation. Nor does it mean ignoring the obvious fact that the USSR is inescapably a European power. But it does mean confronting that division and seeking a way between the poles of the Cold War. It should be added that this is forced upon us. Not to seek nuclear disarmament is to run horrifying risks. To seek nuclear disarmament is to seek an alternative to Cold War in Europe. If we want at least to reduce the immediate risks, we must press towards identifying a long-term alternative to the politics which have created those risks. Whether the disarmament movements are 'neutralist' as American government spokespeople assert is arguable. But that they must eventually seek a changed relationship to each of the superpowers is in the end undeniable.

The goal of European nuclear disarmament is essentially very simple. Yet it is also extremely complex. It should now be clear why that is the case: it goes straight to the heart of a very complex matter, the post-1945 division of Europe, the shape of relations between the superpowers and Europe for over thirty years. And it does that at a time when in both East and West those relations and the system of which they are a part are in crisis. Within this, there are further degrees of complexity relating to the weapons themselves, the strategies they apply to, the relationships they embody and the various possible approaches to the task of eliminating them. END has not provided all the answers, nor would we claim that this book has all the answers. Indeed, what is most exciting about the disarmament movements is the ferment of ideas as people face and think through problems, learning from each other's very different experiences and perspectives. It is not only people that are in motion in Western Europe, but also thought. As we clarify the problems, so we shall together clarify the solutions. This book is a contribution to that process.

NOTES

1. Caspar Weinberger, Statement before the Senate Armed Services Committee, March 4, 1981 (mimeo), p. 1.
2. The END Appeal is reproduced in E.P. Thompson & D. Smith, (eds.), *Protest and Survive* (Penguin, 1980).
3. K. Coates, 'For a Nuclear-free Europe', in *Protest and Survive.*

Part I:

Arming Europe

NUCLEAR STRATEGY AND TECHNOLOGY

Allan Krass and Dan Smith

In the attempt to understand nuclear strategy and new developments in the field of nuclear weapons, the term 'deterrence' now serves as much to cause confusion as to enlighten. In western countries, the popular conception of deterrence is that it is fundamentally defensive and reactive: nuclear weapons would be used by the West only in retaliation, and are possessed only so that the threat of overwhelming retaliation will deter aggression.

However, there are several different doctrines for nuclear weapons which can all be referred to under the label of deterrence. The concept has undergone continual and profound changes over the past three decades. The doctrines which have now emerged are barely distinguishable from the coercive strategies of threat and counter-threat which have characterised the politics of the industrialised world for over a century—with the crucial exception, of course, that the armed forces to which they relate now possess vastly more destructive power.

Through the tangled web of different doctrines all calling themselves 'deterrence' it is possible to distinguish two basic models. One is the reactive and defensive strategy popularly understood to be the intrinsic nature of nuclear deterrence— we shall refer to this as 'pure' deterrence. The other is a more complex and flexible approach to the question of the use of nuclear weapons and can be referred to as a 'war-fighting' doctrine or 'counterforce' strategy (so-called because of the importance it gives to destroying the other side's *forces*). Like pure deterrence, war-fighting or counterforce strategies mount a threat to a potential aggressor which is intended to deter that aggressor, but the nature of the threat is different. At its most direct, we can say that the threat entailed in pure deterrence is a threat of *punishment,* while the threat entailed in counter force strategy is a threat of *defeat.* Defeat for one side implies victory for the other: thus it is necessary to prepare to fight and win a nuclear war. Pure deterrence is not interested in victory, only in inflicting annihilation on the aggressor whatever annihilation the deterring state has itself suffered.

The basic difference between punishment and defeat is reflected in different doctrines about the employment of and the requirements for nuclear weapons. Pure deterrence supposes that nuclear weapons would only be used in retaliation for a nuclear attack, and, seeking to inflict enormous damage in return, requires powerful 'city-killing' weapons with no very stringent demands in terms of accuracy. By contrast, a counterforce or war-fighting strategy is more flexible: nuclear weapons might be used in retaliation, but they might be used before the other side has launched a nuclear strike; they might be used in overwhelming force, or in relatively limited ways; it is therefore necessary to have a wide range of types of weapons, and to have the greatest accuracy possible.

In this context, it should be noted that for as long as NATO has had nuclear weapons in Europe (since the early 1950s) it has reserved the option of using them whether or not the Warsaw Pact has already launched nuclear strikes. NATO's doctrine of deterrence, that is, includes the willingness to retaliate with nuclear means against non-nuclear aggression, and thus to start a nuclear war. Similarly, in the 1950s and again in the 1970s and today, US doctrine for strategic nuclear forces has included the possible 'first use' of nuclear weapons.

In this essay we shall first look at the problems of pure deterrence. These problems are partly due to flaws and contradictions within the theory of nuclear deterrence itself, partly the result of pressures on deterrence in practice. One of the major pressures comes from the seemingly irresistible onward march of technology, constantly creating problems for deterrence, constantly making available strategic options which seem to make counterforce more attractive. We shall then consider the flaws in counterforce strategy, the immense

4

risks that are taken on the basis of elaborate theories which seem simply to ignore the problems and dangers they are generating. And then we shall turn to a summary of the technological developments of the 1970s which have all moved nuclear doctrine towards counterforce.

In fact, we must begin by realising that pure nuclear deterrence has never really been practised, although the doctrine of 'mutual assured destruction' in the USA in the 1960s came close to it. But the popular conception of deterrence as essentially defensive and reactive has been reinforced by numerous statements and writings, of which one stands out as having particular historical significance, made by the USA's Secretary of State, John Foster Dulles, in 1954:[1]

> The way to deter aggression is for the free community to be willing and able to respond vigorously at places and with means of its own choosing. . . to depend primarily on a great capacity to retaliate instantly, by means and at places of our choosing.

Similarly, on the Soviet side, also in 1954:[2]

> If, however, the aggressive circles, relying on atomic weapons, should decide on madness and seek to test the strength and might of the Soviet Union, then it cannot be doubted that the aggressor would be crushed by that very weapon. . .

These statements leave no doubt that deterrence is a system based on threat. But to understand how deterrence has shifted since 1954, it is essential to understand the dual nature of threats: they can be defensive or offensive, deterrent or coercive.

It would be impossible to explain the development of modern nuclear weapons if one insisted on defining deterrence as purely defensive and reactive. We must now learn to think of deterrence as 'flexible' and 'extended', containing capabilities for 'second-strike counterforce' and 'sub-holocaust engagements'. It has come to be accepted in the USA that nuclear deterrence must be addressed to threats far below the level of destructiveness of strategic nuclear warfare, and

5

some writers close to the Reagan administration have been willing to go further:[3]

> (T)he West needs to devise ways in which it can employ strategic nuclear forces coercively, while minimizing the potentially paralyzing impact of self-deterrence. US strategic planning should exploit Soviet fears insofar as is feasible from the Soviet perspective. . .

Soviet views are more difficult to ascertain; but they seem to have been more consistent and less ambiguous (at least on the surface) than American views. Most interpreters of Soviet nuclear doctrines agree that the USSR has never made much of an intellectual effort to distinguish between concepts of deterrence and war-fighting. The Soviet Union has certainly recognised the deterrent value of its military power, but appears to have assumed that this arises ultimately from its power to fight and win wars. Whether a western interpreter chooses to focus on the deterrent or the war-fighting aspect seems to depend more on the political preferences of the observer than on any inherent doctrinal distinction or preference in Soviet thinking itself.

THE PROBLEMS OF PURE DETERRENCE

On the face of it, 'pure' deterrence seems to hold out a relatively benevolent prospect, in which the states of both NATO and the Warsaw Pact would be deterred from nuclear aggression. If this could be extended to cover non-nuclear aggression (although it would be preferable to deter non-nuclear aggression through non-nuclear means), it would seem that a stable situation of mutual deterrence and mutual non-aggression would result. This would not be the best of all possible worlds—the system might break down and lead to war through technical accident, miscalculation or sheer mischance, but it might be argued that technological safeguards together with political dialogue and the 'hot-line' system of crisis-communications could sharply reduce those risks. It would seem to provide a way of living with nuclear weapons in a divided world, and it might provide the basis for steadily reducing nuclear weapons by mutual agreement.

Many advocates of nuclear arms control and most of those

who believe the West's nuclear strategies are strategies of pure deterrence seem to believe that this is an accurate picture of the present. To understand why it is not accurate one needs to understand the problems of pure deterrence, problems which have been exposed by critics on two sides—by those who have gone on to argue for nuclear disarmament, and by those who have gone on to argue for different doctrines for the deployment of nuclear weapons.

The first problem is the essentially defensive and reactive nature of a pure deterrent posture. Looked at one way, this seems like its basic attraction, the foundation on which the stability of mutual deterrence could be built. But looked at differently, it results in a strategy which leaves all the initiative to the adversary and deprives the possession of nuclear weapons of any real political value: in a purely deterrent posture, nuclear weapons become useless as coercive implements. In the USA, this criticism had been thoroughly aired even before the first public enunciation of the doctrine of massive retaliation in 1954. Indeed, in the same speech, from which we have already quoted, Dulles took pains to reassure his audience that the new doctrine did not abandon the initiative to the other side:

> Now the Department of Defense and the Joint Chiefs of Staff can shape our military establishment to fit. . . *our* policy, instead of having to try to be ready to meet the enemy's many choices. That permits. . . a selection of military means instead of a multiplication of means. . .

But these reassurances were not convincing then, and they are not convincing today.

The second problem is suggested by the requirement that, to be deterred, the enemy 'must understand what behaviour of his will cause the violence to be inflicted and what will cause it to be withheld'.[4] In other words, the deterrent threat must be both unambiguous and credible. But by being unambiguous, by being explicit about just what is being deterred, and by making an irrevocable commitment to carrying out the threat, a national leader totally loses flexibility; this is a position in which no political leader will

7

ever willingly be placed, and which again risks ceding the initiative to the adversary. The criterion of credibility proved too full of logical flaws to survive analysis. Simply stated, the problem is how a nation credibly commits itself to retaliation by suicide, to saying, in effect, 'One step further and I'll shoot (myself).' Attempts to solve this problem led to some of the more bizarre proposals of the 1950s in the form of 'doomsday machines' which would automatically unleash nuclear retaliation against the appropriate form of aggression. Early on, it was recognised that assigning the task of retaliation to computers could eliminate the unpredictable factors of human fear, remorse or compassion.

The third problem is revealed exactly by such proposals, which carry pure deterrence to its full technological and logical conclusions: its utter moral repugnance. Naturally, this was initially exposed more by advocates of disarmament than by advocates of war-fighting concepts, but the latter have also often relied on moral objections to mass murder to sustain their arguments. It is a measure of the way in which the debate has shifted that, especially in the USA, advocates of arms control and disarmament now find themselves often forced to defend, on practical political grounds, a strategy based on threats to destroy civilian populations which fundamentally conflicts with their own moral convictions.

The fourth problem follows from these three—the effect of deterrence on the morale of the political leadership, military establishment and civilian population. The morale of political leaders cannot help but be reduced by a strategy which effectively puts the most vital issues of security beyond their control and commits them to mass murder, while civilian morale must certainly be undermined by a strategy which leaves civilians as helpless victims of a constantly threatening destruction against which defence is both impossible and (if the doctrine is taken seriously) undesirable. But equally important would be the effect on military morale. A pure deterrent posture would put the military into an impossible position: it recognises the possibility of war and, indeed, postulates the adversary's aggressive predilections, but then leaves all the initiative to that adversary to decide when, where and how the war will be fought. The doctrine would

8

deny the possibility or desirability of pre-empting, weakening or resisting the attack and, in effect, say to military officers: You must sit and wait for the enemy to attack; then you must sit and watch the enemy's missiles destroy your planes, ships, missiles, communications facilities and so on; then your job is to gather together everything you have left and send it off to kill defenceless civilians in the enemy's country; the more defenceless civilians you kill, the better you will have done your job; if the enemy kills defenceless civilians in your country, that is not your concern and is irrelevant to the completion of your task.

These four problems in pure deterrence constitute strong arguments against it. But a fifth problem, concerning technological advance, makes it extremely difficult to sustain a stable basis for deterrence. Pure deterrence might be expected to create stability between two adversaries, and to some extent this stability is necessary for the continuation of mutual deterrence. But the world does not actually stand still. Developments in technology make new capabilities available to the military on each side, and thus also provide new problems for the other. Thus, improved missile accuracy has fuelled the debate in the USA about the vulnerability to a Soviet strike of American inter-continental ballistic missiles, providing the justification for the concept of mobile basing for the new M-X missile. The invulnerability of submarine-launched missiles may be open to question as the counter-measures and counter-counter-measures of anti-submarine warfare develop apace. Anti-satellite technologies raise doubts about the survivability of satellite-based communications and therefore about the ability even to order, let alone plan and coordinate a retaliatory strike. Each new development demands a response (and then a counter-response), so that there can never be a fixed answer to the famous question which poses the central issue of planning for nuclear deterrence—How much is enough?[5]

At one level, pure deterrence demands continual technological innovation, to provide ever re-strengthened deterrence against the adversary's developing capabilities. Yet this continual process of innovation consistently undermines pure deterrence, as the adversary responds in turn. At the same time, of course, technology is also driven forward, not by rational strategic calculation (or any kind of strategic calculation), but by the institutional interests around the technologies. These, the corporations in the USA and design bureaux in the USSR, in alliance with groups within the military, bureaucratic and political leadership can only justify their continued existence by continued innovation. And this process of innovation, whether it is marginal or providing technological breakthroughs, provides new possibilities in nuclear planning. Critically, in the 1970s technological developments have offered the possibility of thinking about nuclear weapons in a different light, the temptation to move away from pure deterrence and the constraints of passivity and inflexibility into more flexible fields.

If these arguments are correct, and pure deterrence is unsatisfactory over the long term, what are the alternatives? Clearly, they are either nuclear disarmament or the adoption of a more 'flexible' approach to nuclear deterrence, leading into strategies which prepare for nuclear warfare, for fighting and winning it. There can be little doubt which course the superpowers have taken.

THE LURE OF COUNTERFORCE

As the term implies, counterforce targeting is a policy of targeting nuclear forces against the armed forces (especially nuclear) of the other side. The opposite form of targeting would be counter-city. American doctrine also refers to counter-value or countervailing targeting, which embraces both counterforce and counter-city.

It is essential to understand at the outset that American nuclear strategy has always included counterforce targeting, under the doctrines of massive retaliation and mutual assured destruction in the 1950s and 1960s no less than under the doctrines of the 1970s and now. A counterforce *strategy*, however, is one which emphasises the element of counterforce targeting and links it to the concepts of limited nuclear war-fighting which now abound in western strategic circles. It is distinct from the notion of pure deterrence we have just been discussing, but it does not exclude deterrence. It is both easy and intellectually respectable to argue that the deterrent function is a product of the ability to fight a nuclear war and win it. But, as we noted at the outset, the basic deterrent threat is different: it is the threat of defeat, not of simple punishment. And the deterrent function as such becomes conceptually less distinctive and effectively more incidental to the primary war-fighting function.

The pursuit of a nuclear counterforce strategy derives from a continuing desire to make nuclear weapons useful as instruments of war, coupled with an understanding, either explicit or implicit, of the inadequacies of pure deterrence. So the attractions of counterforce are to some extent the mirror images of the deficiencies of deterrence, but there is a significant additional set of motivations which have to do with an undiminished belief in the utility of military force in international affairs and an unquestioned faith that the most powerful weapon ever invented must be capable of making a major contribution to this utility.

The desire to make nuclear weapons militarily useful is as old as the weapon itself. The first major doctrinal battles within the US government were being fought even as the public was adjusting to the new idea that nuclear weapons had made future wars 'unthinkable'. In fact they were as thinkable as ever, and the discussion of how nuclear weapons were to be employed quickly accommodated itself to the political environment of the US military. The battle lines were drawn between air power enthusiasts in the Air Force and the traditional Army-Navy hierarchy.

The argument was not about counterforce versus deterrence, but about different conceptions of the best counterforce applications of the new weapons. The US Air Force attempted to gain a monopoly control over nuclear weapons by stressing their usefulness in strategic attacks on the enemy heartland, while the Army emphasised their potential for battlefield use.

However ardently the US Air Force may have wished for a counterforce mission in the 1940s and 1950s, technological, economic and political constraints produced a strategic posture which looked much more like deterrence. But the deterrence doctrine was then, as it has been ever since, a doctrine of necessity, enforced more by technological

11

constraints than by any desire to renounce counterforce as a viable military posture. The persistence of the search for a counterforce capability can be traced through all US Administrations. In the Kennedy Administration Robert McNamara, Secretary of Defense, promoted the concept of 'damage limitation' or 'no-cities' warfare. This proposed that, after nuclear deterrence had failed and nuclear war begun, it would be possible to limit damage to the USA by refraining from attacking Soviet cities and thus holding them 'hostage', continuing the war meanwhile by counterforce attacks.[6] When McNamara came to understand the technological limitations which made 'damage limitation' unworkable, he set in motion a determined effort to overcome them, opting in the interim for the doctrine of 'mutual assured destruction' —the embodiment of the balance of terror in US nuclear strategy.

Richard Nixon came to Washington as President, advocating 'superiority' over the USSR; the subsequent softening of this word to 'sufficiency' had more of a cosmetic than an operational significance. The leadership of Melvin Laird and James Schlesinger in the Pentagon carried on the development of counterforce capabilities, leading to the declaration of a strategy of limited options—that is, options for the limited use of nuclear weapons—by Schlesinger in January 1974. Under the Presidency of James Carter, Harold Brown at the Pentagon continued this basic thrust, formally codified by the release of Presidential Directive 59 in summer 1980.[7] Counterforce thinking, planning and weapons procurement were modified only in detail during the Carter-Brown years.

Thus, over the years, it is only the technical means of achieving the mission which have from time to time been re-evaluated: the mission itself has not been questioned. There seems very little likelihood that it will be questioned under Reagan.

The USSR has moved along a similar course. It would appear that in the battle for the post-Stalin leadership in the 1950s, arguments about nuclear deterrence were instrumental in Nikita Khrushchev's successful efforts to oust Premier Malenkov. With the support of the Soviet Army, Khrushchev argued that pure or 'minimal' deterrence would lead to

12

'complacency' and 'defeatism' and that it was essential for Soviet foreign policy to maintain the belief that defence was possible and nuclear war was winnable. But this was followed by Khrushchev's own adoption of 'minimal' deterrence, which may have been a genuine doctrinal preference on his part, or merely a concession to the USSR's technological limitations.[8] In any case, the counterforce course has certainly been followed by the USSR, and with considerable vigour, in the years since the fall of Khrushchev.

However, it is still possible to identify important differences between US and Soviet doctrines. The growing American emphasis on limited nuclear wars involving counterforce targeting was clearly stated by James Schlesinger in 1975:[9]

> In answering the question, 'Do you think it is possible to have a limited nuclear war, just to exchange a couple of weapons?' the Secretary said, 'I believe so.' He added it is easier to think of the circumstances in which limited use might occur than it would be to think of a massive all-out strike against the urban industrial base of another nation, which has the capability of striking back.

And although, as Defense Secretary, Harold Brown made it clear that he thought there could be no guarantee that a limited nuclear war would remain limited, he continued to assert the need for the USA to have options for the limited use of nuclear weapons—that is, for limited nuclear war.[10] It is clear that a preponderance of US military and civilian strategists favour this approach, but no similar tendency can be identified in Soviet strategic declarations, and this is naturally a matter of some concern to US strategists. The Soviet reaction to the enunciation of the strategy of limited options in 1974 was uniformly hostile, and included the criticism that the strategy was insensitive to the realities of nuclear warfare. This reaction, moreover, was well in keeping with the main lines of long-standing Soviet doctrine on nuclear war which is, as one writer has noted, 'a highly institutionalized body of official precepts':[11]

> Soviet military writings continue to assert that in any nuclear engagement, theatre or global, Soviet nuclear forces will strike

13

simultaneously at the strategic capabilities, political-military command infrastructure, and economic-administrative centers of the adversary. Moreover, they reveal no trace of interest in the notions of intrawar bargaining, graduated escalation, and crisis management which play a heavy role in current US strategic theorizing.

In the face of this unfortunately intransigent refusal to play the counterforce game, the American hope seems to be that improvements in Soviet technology will tempt the USSR into playing this game according to American rules. As two influential American analysts have put it.[12]

> Russian commentators once scoffed at the idea that there could be a substantial conflict in the NATO area that would not immediately become nuclear. After much invective on the subject, they eventually admitted the need to plan for nonnuclear engagements. For good reason, we might witness the same phenomenon with respect to other forms of limitation, for example, within nuclear conflict. Now a great deal of Soviet rhetoric flows about the absurdity of the notion of limiting the use of nuclear weapons; on the other hand there is no real evidence that the Soviets would abandon all caution in a nuclear or any other conflict.

On the other hand again, there is 'no real evidence' to support any of this theorising, posturing, procuring and deploying. We do not refer to 'the American *hope*' facetiously: counterforce strategies and options for limited nuclear war are built entirely on hope—that the weapons will work as they are supposed to, that control will be maintained and both sides will keep to the game-plan, that once war starts both sides will somehow recognise a common point where the calculations of cost and benefit balance out so they can both stop the game, but above all else that when it comes to it, when it's 'eyeball to eyeball', 'they' will 'blink' first, and 'we' will win without a shot being fired.

THE PROBLEMS OF COUNTERFORCE

A counterforce strategy may include (as it does now in the West) the option of launching the first nuclear strike, but it is by no means a strategy necessarily based on the launching of an all-out first strike aimed at the total incapacitation of

NUCLEAR STRATEGY & TECHNOLOGY

the enemy's own nuclear forces—a 'disarming first strike', as it is charmingly called in the trade.

Even so, the first defect of counterforce lies precisely here, in the high premium it places, even unintentionally, on a first strike. The weapons and support systems required for a flexible counterforce strategy are indistinguishable from those required for a 'disarming first strike'. Thus, if one side does not trust the other's declared strategy, and looks beneath it to assess the hardware, there will be a great deal of justification in concluding that, if the political situation deteriorates to the point where war seems imminent, it will face an attempt at a 'disarming first strike' against it.

The problem is compounded by the increasingly accurate multiple independently-targeted re-entry vehicles or warheads (MIRVs) which both sides now deploy. MIRVing provides large numbers of warheads on relatively few systems—for example, 160 warheads on each US Poseidon submarine, and as many as 250 or more on each of the planned Trident submarines. Yet it only takes one shot (and not necessarily a nuclear one) to destroy a single submarine. In principle, one could calculate that the USA's 9,000 strategic warheads could be destroyed by about 1,200 well-aimed Soviet warheads, while the USSR's 6,000 strategic warheads might be destroyed by approximately 1,500 successful US shots.[13] Thus the USA has about six times as many warheads as it needs to destroy the Soviet strategic force, and the USSR has about five times as many warheads as it needs to do the same to the USA. The significance of these ratios should not be overstressed, because the success of such an enormously risky and complex enterprise would depend on far more than the simple ratio of warheads to targets.

However, if one assumes high reliability and accuracy for the weapons used in the first strike, the ratios do reveal a growing disparity between the losses which will be suffered by the side which strikes first and the losses which will be suffered by the side which strikes second. Accordingly, if each side has forces which, whatever the declaratory doctrine, reveal a potential for a disarming first strike, and if war seems imminent, either side may conclude that the other is indeed about to launch a first strike, and therefore conclude it can only cut its losses by launching its own first strike. Either side may conclude that its own only rational option is to 'get its retaliation in first'. As a result, we can only conclude that counterforce strategies weaken deterrence and make war more likely in times of crisis—which are exactly the times when deterrence should be strongest.

The second major problem of a counterforce strategy is its dependence on theories of intra-war bargaining, intra-war deterrence and controlled escalation, theories which have fundamental logical flaws. As it has been put:[14]

> It is the nature of escalation that each move passes the option to the other side, while at the same time the party which seems to be losing will be tempted to keep raising the ante. . . Once on the tiger's back we cannot be sure of picking the place to dismount.

Yet it is integral to the idea of limited nuclear warfare, and to the currently fashionable concept of 'escalation dominance', that we can mount and dismount the tiger at will. There is a surface plausibility in the idea that since each side will be concerned to limit the damage to itself, both sides will be interested in fighting a limited nuclear war rather than a total war. But this plausibility vanishes once one tries to identify the moment at which one side would decide to leave the other with the final say, the final shot. And if it therefore seems likely that neither side will wish to pull out leaving the other with the 'advantage', then why should either side bother with limited war at all? It is surely more likely that both sides would conclude that, since the most likely outcome is a non-limited war, the best option is to make an all-out strike immediately. Despite the pseudo-scientific appearance of theories of intra-war bargaining, they lack all rational foundation. And their irrationality is merely emphasised by the lack of interest in such theories displayed by the USSR.

A third flaw in the logic of counterforce lies in the requirement for efficient, reliable and speedy performance of assigned missions involving high accuracy. Despite remarkable progress in counterforce capabilities, doubts must remain about this requirement. Reminders of military and technological fallibility recur with alarming regularity: the failure of the US rescue mission in Iran, the false alerts generated by the US warning system, and the recent revelation that for 18 months in the 1960s most of the warheads on US Polaris submarines were inoperative.[15]

An article in 1980, based on interviews with knowledgeable ex-officials in the US military establishment, argued that the accuracies claimed for inter-continental nuclear missiles are exaggerated.[16] The argument may be somewhat overstated (too easily dismissing counterforce capabilities and the potential vulnerability of submarines) but it provides a firm basis for scepticism about the public claims of accuracy and reliability made by the military. Most tellingly, inter-continental missiles have never been tested over their expected wartime flight courses. US missiles are tested on an east-west track from California to the Marshall Islands in the Pacific, while Soviet missiles are tested west-east, from west of the Urals to the Kamchatka Peninsula or beyond. Thus, guidance systems have been checked and calibrated over regions of the Earth with different gravitational anomalies from the regions over which they would fly in war. And while US and Soviet geodetic and other satellites have been mapping the gravitational field for many years, it requires a substantial leap of faith to believe that a missile can be given pinpoint accuracy over a range of 10,000 kilometres on the very first shot simply by programming this information into its guidance computer.

It may be argued that these problems are purely technical, and therefore amenable to ultimate, if not imminent, technical solution. Reliability is another matter. The history of military technology is a history of poorly designed equipment, slovenly maintenance and regular breakdowns. Moreover, however limited the planned nuclear strike, the stakes in ordering it would be so great that it is hard to imagine a national leader doing so unless the situation were desperate. But in a desperate situation, thoughts will turn to massive strikes rather than limited ones: saturation is the traditional military remedy for doubts about accuracy and reliability.

The logic of counterforce is therefore undermined by a series of other inter-locking logics of far greater plausibility. Counterforce strategies require the precise, surgical use of

17

nuclear weapons, but for several reasons, some of them technical, nuclear weapons cannot be scalpels—they are sledgehammers, and the danger is that far too many strategists and political leaders appear to be dreaming these massive, blunt instruments could actually be used with surgical delicacy. It can be added, however, that the entire counter-force posture is based on weapons and theories which have never been tested under the conditions in which they will have to be used. While generals have often been accused of preparing to fight the last war, preparations are now being made to fight a war in which the old process of learning by trial and error is impracticable. This is certainly one major reason why nuclear weapons have not been used since Nagasaki over 35 years ago. The non-use precedent grows stronger with the passing of time, and presents even greater obstacles to plans for the controlled use of nuclear weapons. It is an essential part of the 'self-deterrence' which most of us find comforting, but which many analysts find increasingly inconvenient.

DEVELOPMENTS IN COUNTERFORCE TECHNOLOGY

One may note the evident weaknesses and dangers of a counterforce strategy; one may note the inhibitions on the actual use of nuclear weapons: yet one cannot ignore the development of weapon systems suited to a counterforce strategy emphasising the utility of nuclear weapons. It is, indeed, impossible to understand the many technological innovations in nuclear weapons and support systems over the past decade except in the context of the lure of counterforce strategies. Such strategies contemplate a wide range of options and require the hardware to implement them.

The most demanding requirements are for a pre-emptive first strike. Most of an enemy's retaliatory capability must be destroyed quickly and without warning. Offensive weapons must reach their targets very quickly or without being detected; they must be extremely accurate and reliable; they must be varied, since the targets they must strike are varied; they must be available in large numbers to hedge against breakdowns; they must be backed by extensive reconnaissance, surveillance and communications systems

18

for rapid assessment of the attack's success, together with the capability for rapid retargeting of weapons for subsequent strikes. No first strike could possibly be 100 per cent effective, so preparations must be made to protect both military and civilians from retaliation.

For limited nuclear war, these same capabilities are required, but they would probably not be needed all at the same time and perhaps not in quite such profusion. Minimal requirements are reliable, accurate and survivable weapons, anti-submarine capabilities and the protection of military installations. Protection of cities and civilians may also be desirable, although if it is genuinely believed that the two warring sides really would avoid each other's cities then this protection can be less extensive.

Not all aspects of these multiple requirements have been pursued with the same intensity or success during the 1970s, and the relative emphasis on the various aspects differs between the USA and USSR. But the patterns of techno-logical development have been consistent with the deliberate pursuit of counterforce capabilities on both sides. In what follows we briefly review the main developments.[17]

1. Accuracy

The accurate delivery of nuclear missiles against small targets which have been specially strengthened ('hardened') to resist nuclear blast is the most important single element of counter-force war. Accuracy is measured in terms of the 'circular error probable' (CEP): if one assumes the target to be the centre point of a circle, the CEP is the radius of that circle within which, all things being equal, 50 per cent or more of the warheads fired at that target would land. The CEP is thus a calculation of statistical probability. In considering CEPs, therefore, it is important to keep in mind, first, that pro-bability does not mean certainty; second, that is also probable that warheads will land further away from the target than the distance of the CEP; and, third, that the accuracy has probably been exaggerated.

With these reservations in mind, we can note that in 1972 the best US missiles had CEPs of about 500 metres while the best Soviet CEPs were under 1,500 metres.[18] American

19

counterforce capabilities against hardened targets were only marginally effective for land-based inter-continental ballistic missiles (ICBMs) and far less effective for submarine-launched ballistic missiles (SLBMs); the USSR lacked a significant capability against hard targets. At the end of the 1970s the situation had changed considerably with the installation of the NS-20 guidance system on the US Minuteman III ICBM, reducing the CEP to 200 metres.[19] A CEP comparable to this has been attributed to the USSR's SS-18 ICBM;[20] although western estimates of Soviet capabilities have been known to exaggerate, the question of whether or not the particular estimate of SS-18's accuracy is reliable is less important than the evidence that the USSR has significantly improved its missiles' accuracies during the 1970s. There is no reason to doubt either the USSR's intention or capability to make further improvements in the 1980s.

These improvements in accuracy have required improved design of warheads, and will be taken further by the current development of terminal guidance and manoeuvrable warheads. These, intended for the next generation of weapons, such as the American M-X missile now being developed, could lead to CEPs of well under 100 metres. Also instrumental in improving accuracy have been improvements in satellite technology, both to provide precision mapping of launch-points and targets, and to provide mid-course guidance for the 'MIRV buses' which carry the warheads through space before they re-enter the earth's atmosphere. New navigational aids are enabling submarines to locate their positions more precisely, thus improving the accuracy of SLBMs, the new generation of which (Trident) can be considered counterforce weapons.

These developments are removing the single most important technological obstacle to using strategic nuclear weapons against hardened targets. Their existence and aim was already revealed in 1970 by General Ryan, Chief of Staff of the US Air Force, who was quoted as saying:[21]

> We have a programme we are pushing to increase the yield of our warheads and decrease the circular error probable, so that we have what we call a hard-target killer, which we do not have in the inventory at the present moment.

20

The statement was repudiated by President Nixon who denied such a programme existed; subsequent years have shown General Ryan's statement was correct. By the end of the 1970s, the USA's Minuteman II missiles had an 80 per cent probability of destroying with a single shot a well-hardened Soviet missile silo. Current developments will push that percentage higher.

2. Anti-submarine warfare (ASW)

If the threat to fight nuclear war is to be credible, something has to be done to neutralise the enemy's missile-launching submarines. Each submarine may carry from 12 to 24 missiles, with possibly up to 14 accurate and independently-targeted warheads on each missile; a single submarine represents what most people might consider an effective deterrent capability. But a single submarine or a small number would not be effective in fighting a prolonged war, since once a submarine has fired its first missile it has revealed a great deal about its location. Unless it fires all its missiles quickly it makes itself highly vulnerable to ASW. Accordingly, were it possible drastically to reduce the enemy's missile-launching submarine force in an initial attack, and then follow it up with rapid attrition, the enemy's war-fighting capability would be seriously damaged. If either side possessed such an ASW capability, the submarine 'deterrent' would lose its vaunted invulnerability.

At the start of the 1970s, there seemed little danger that this strategic ASW capability could be developed. But in 1978 the US Congressional Research Service suggested that the USA's superiority in digital computer technology and electronics could be providing nuclear-powered submarines with the[22]

capability to trail Soviet submarines without their knowledge, and if detected to maintain trail against even a determined and uncooperative Soviet commanding officer.

Even the need for trailing enemy missile-launching submarines could be removed if another line of technological development keeps evolving. This includes the stationing of

21

widespread networks of stationary and mobile sonubuoys for detecting, locating and monitoring submarine activity, linked to information-processing technologies capable of converting a vast amount of data into usable form. As these technologies are joined to sophisticated satellite communications systems, the USA, which is well ahead of the USSR in the whole field of ASW, will be able to approach a total and immediate surveillance of the oceans.

Once the problems of detection and location are solved, the rest—destruction—is straightforward, and can be effected by aircraft, hunter-killer submarines or surface vessels. The USA's lead in ASW relates not to the means of destruction, but to the more sophisticated and complex technologies of surveillance and information-processing. In addition, it has the advantage of geography: for access to the oceans, Soviet missile-launching submarines must pass through various choke-points of easily monitored waters, from which point their continued trailing or monitoring is much easier.

It is worth commenting on a further feature of systems for detecting submarines. They are extremely 'soft' targets, easily destroyed or rendered ineffective in a prolonged war, and the cost of introducing back-up systems will almost certainly be greater than the cost for the other side of destroying them. It therefore follows that such systems are best suited to providing warning of or helping coordinate a surprise attack; that is, they are less useful in a counter-force second strike in a limited nuclear war than they are in a pre-emptive first strike.

3. Command, Control, Communications and Intelligence (C³ I)

A nuclear war-fighting strategy, whether for an all-out first strike, or a limited nuclear engagement, demands a highly sophisticated and flexible $C^3 I$ system for coordinating the employment of nuclear weapons and instantaneously assessing the effects of their use. A state entering a nuclear war with any confidence of confining its scope to limited objectives would require, as a pre-condition, considerable confidence that its weapons would be delivered accurately, that close control could be maintained over all forces, that rapid and

22

reliable assessment of damage to both the enemy's and its own forces could be maintained, and that communications to the enemy were kept open for the speedy transmission of unambiguous messages.

The 1970s have seen impressive technological progress in two areas essential to these preconditions. The first is the development of 'packet-switching' techniques: this involves breaking down data into conveniently sized packages for transmission by the quickest of several possible routes; at the receiving end, a computer can then reassemble the data into their proper order.[23] This permits vast amounts of data, gathered in a variety of ways, to be absorbed and utilised so that tactical decisions can be made swiftly and with full information. It would be especially important in anti-submarine warfare, but necessary also for orchestrating other operations. The second development contributes to the security and reliability of communications through the so-called 'spread spectrum' technologies. These make it possible to transmit coded messages across a range of frequencies, making them extremely difficult to jam or listen in to.[24] While the basic concepts have been used for over 20 years, it is only the recent development of digital components and devices which have made them practicable for widespread application.

Between them, these two developments contribute considerably to the capability for a counterforce attack and for limited nuclear war: improved data-handling will speed up the process of gathering and evaluating information on targets and damage, while the ability to send unjammable and secure messages will increase the reliability and flexibility of control over forces and weapons. The goal of monitoring the 'battlefield' (however that might be defined) and gaining instantaneous knowledge of developments is pursued largely by means of space-based reconnaissance systems. Steady progress was recorded in the 1970s in improving electromagnetic sensors for satellites. Improvements in processing and transmitting data obviously promise much swifter use of satellite information.

The relevance of this rapid acquisition of information for decision making is underlined by substantial improvements in the ability to retarget missiles. Here the main landmark was in the early 1970s, when the USA introduced the Command Data Buffer system, which makes it possible to retarget the entire US force of Minuteman III land-based intercontinental missiles in ten hours, a task which used to take weeks.[25]

These developments are all impressive, especially when considered in their combination with a vast array of communications facilities, based on land, at sea and in space. But measured against the missions they would be asked to perform, they fall far short of their goals. This may be more to do with the inherent implausibility of the missions, than with any technical shortcoming as such; in the end, however good the information and the technology, the kind of control demanded by counterforce will always be political, strategic and tactical, and no technology can eliminate the uncertainties which reside there. In addition, there was evidence by the end of the 1970s that existing systems of reconnaissance, communications and control could be much less effective than had been thought. There have, for example, been the revelations of the false alerts generated by the US attack-warning systems. Obviously, the more that the USA's and USSR's strategic doctrines and weapons programmes are guided by counterforce, the more dangerous such false alerts will become.

In addition to the problem of reliability, there is the problem of survivability. As with ASW detection systems, so with C^3I facilities, there is a problem of their inherent 'softness'. Along with their absolute necessity for effective war fighting, this makes them prime targets for early attack. This is highly relevant to the question of deterrence and counterforce: the more vulnerable a state's C^3I system is, the stronger is its incentive to strike first if war seems inevitable.

4. Anti-satellite warfare (ASAT)
All of our comments above indicate the growing importance of satellites to war-fighting. It is therefore hardly surprising to find the development of techniques for destroying the enemy's satellites. To some degree, the problems of ASAT are opposite to those of anti-submarine warfare, in which the

major problem is detection and tracking, after which destruction is fairly straightforward. In ASAT, detection and tracking is not difficult, but destruction is, especially if it must be done quickly and in coordination with other military operations.

There are two basic methods of ASAT: 'direct ascent' (i.e., shooting down the target satellite with a missile launched from Earth) and 'orbital rendezvous' (i.e., destroying the target satellite by means of another satellite which approaches the target, identifies it and then explodes). These techniques have been worked on since the 1960s when the USA first deployed land-based ASAT nuclear missiles.[26] The USA has experimented with 'orbital rendezvous' techniques, but its current preference appears to be for 'direct ascent'; efforts are in hand to produce a non-nuclear ASAT interceptor equipped with an infra-red homing device to guide it to its target.[27] On the other hand, during the 1970s the USSR revived testing of 'orbital rendezvous' techniques, which seem to be its preference. These two techniques may be supplemented in the future, if the technologies can be perfected, by space-based ASAT laser weapons.[28]

There are many similarities between ASAT (especially in the case of 'direct ascent') and anti-ballistic missiles (ABM) systems. ABM deployment was limited by two US-Soviet arms limitation agreements in the 1970s, and the USA ended its own ABM deployment in the 1970s for technical and domestic political reasons. But research and development continued, and as the 1970s drew to a close, there was renewed interest in the USA in reviving ABM.[29] It is not unreasonable to assume that the two capabilities are being developed in parallel.

5. Intermediate-range systems

The developments we have considered so far have mainly been appropriate for the consideration of counterforce strategy in relation to the central strategic systems of the USA and USSR for inter-continental warfare. However, the events which have done most to fuel the public debates in Europe since late 1979 have related to European theatre nuclear forces, especially intermediate-range systems such as the SS-20 and the Backfire bomber on the Soviet side, and the planned NATO deployment of Tomahawk ground-launched cruise missiles and Pershing II ballistic missiles.

In a certain sense, the developments we have discussed already are equally relevant to these systems. Thus, the Soviet SS-20, equipped with MIRV, replaces the older SS-4 and SS-5 intermediate-range missiles of the USSR. It is credited with high accuracy and a rapid reload capability, and is mounted on a vehicle providing mobility on the ground. It has been widely used as the rationale for the American deployment of Pershing II, which itself exploits improved warhead design and terminal guidance for high accuracy. It should be noted that the SS-20 and Pershing II are not strictly comparable: the SS-20 has a much greater range and carries three warheads to Pershing II's single warhead; on the other hand, the SS-20 can hit targets anywhere in western Europe (and also in China) but not in the USA, whereas the Pershing II, 108 of which are planned for deployment in West Germany, would be able to hit targets in the USSR. It can be added that considerable doubt has been cast on the validity of using the SS-20 to justify deployment of Pershing II or GLCM, partly because of evidence suggesting the SS-20's capabilities have been much over-rated[30] (though by any estimate it remains a powerful weapon), and partly because of evidence suggesting the US Army has been motivated by military and bureaucratic concerns quite detached from any demonstrated or projected Soviet capabilities.[31] In the end, however, both SS-20 and Pershing II are in line with the main direction of developments in nuclear weapons through the 1970s, and in that sense are both comparable and related.

GLCM present a rather more ambiguous case. They are but one variant—the ground-launched one—of the general category of long-range cruise missiles (LRCM), which can also be launched from aircraft, submarines and surface ships. Cruise missile technology represents one of the major technological developments of the 1970s, although the basic principle of an unmanned aircraft flying under power almost all the way to the target (rather than on a pre-set trajectory as with ballistic missiles) is not new. LRCM are essentially computer-age versions of the German V-1 flying-bomb, variously known also as the 'doodlebug' or 'buzz bomb'. They have been made possible by three different strands of technological advance. Advances in aeroengine technology have produced small, light and highly efficient engines; these allied to more energetic liquid fuels increase the range and payload available for small missiles. And solid-state electronics have made new light guidance and control systems possible with high accuracy. The Tomahawk GLCM, of which 464 are planned to be deployed in western Europe, are small (14 feet long and 21 inches in diameter), mounted four at a time on special vehicles to give them mobility on the ground, and are claimed to have a CEP of about 30 metres after flights of up to 2,000 kilometres.

This high accuracy is provided by a system which matches the contours of the territory over which it is flying to a pre-programmed contour map, supplemented at the end of the flight by terminal guidance. It would seem to provide the precision which is ideally suited both to a disarming counter-force first strike and to the conduct of a limited counterforce war. But the missile is relatively slow (sub-sonic speed) and would take some hours to reach its target. Moreover, although its small size would make it hard to detect, once detected it could be shot down. This must reduce its effectiveness as a first strike weapon. When LRCM were first debated in the specialist literature, it was argued that although they could be shot down, they were cheap enough to produce in large numbers (current US plans are for nearly 4,000 LRCM), and could overwhelm enemy defences by saturation. This, however, would seem to undermine the possibility of limiting the nuclear war. At the same time, the high accuracy of LRCM would be unnecessary if their targets were to be cities under a pure deterrent strategy, and their vulnerability remains the same whether they are launched in a first or a retaliatory strike.

It is therefore unclear exactly what role GLCM are intended for. No convincing justification for their deployment has yet been found, although one could speculate that saturating the defence could be an important part of a major first strike, as long as their launching could be properly coordinated with other elements of the total strike. Their usefulness in this role could be increased by shortening their flight-time; work on a supersonic cruise missile with just this end in mind is already in progress in the USA.[32]

6. Developments in the 1980s

Current research and development efforts and plans for weapons procurement indicate that the main lines of the developments in the 1970s summarised above will be continued in the 1980s.

In the USA, the installation of the NS-20 guidance system and Mark 12-A warhead on Minuteman II missiles is in progress, providing unprecedented accuracies. It is possible that further refinement of Minuteman IIIs, possibly using manoeuvreable re-entry vehicles, will go ahead, either alongside the new M-X inter-continental missiles or instead of them. There appears to be some doubt about the worth of the M-X in the USA, especially because of the huge expense of the project (over $50,000 million and possibly over $100,000 million). This massive cost is in part due to the requirement that the M-X should have a mobile basing mode, with each missile rotating at random among a number of fixed silos, in order to complicate the task of a Soviet counter-force strike.

For the sea-based nuclear force, the development of Trident II missiles, utilising stellar guidance and manoeuvrable re-entry vehicles, could provide submarine-launched missiles just as accurate as the ground-launched missiles by the end of the 1980s. This will increase the USA's counterforce capabilities by a large factor.

Deployment of all versions of the long-range cruise missile is planned for the 1980s. Air-launched cruise missiles are currently planned for deployment on B-52 bombers; if the so-called 'stealth' technologies can be developed to make long-range bombers harder to detect by existing radar or infra-red warning systems, the result will be yet another increment for counterforce strength.

Soviet efforts appear to focus on continuing improvements to guidance systems for ballistic missiles. One new missile under development has been described as carrying 10 MIRV warheads, each with a yield of 500 kilotons, a range of 10,000 kilometres, and a CEP of 260 metres.[33] So far, it appears that the USSR has not opted to follow the American example, with the planned M-X, of mobile basing for inter-continental missiles, choosing instead to go for extremely well hardened silos for storing the new missiles. American statements about the accuracy of Soviet missiles should be taken with a grain or two of salt, but even after that it is clear that the USSR is moving in the direction of increased counterforce capability.

In anti-submarine warfare, the USA's goal of instantaneous monitoring of the world's oceans will require increasing sophistication and application of the technologies we have already described. Because of its geography, the USSR faces more obstacles in pursuing such a programme, particularly where it involves deploying fixed ASW monitoring devices. This suggests the USSR will try to rely more heavily on mobile monitoring systems, and since it faces a substantial American technological lead, it will probably make a high priority out of research and development in this area.

In anti-satellite warfare, it seems as if both the USA and USSR will continue to develop along their different ASAT paths. At the moment, the dictum appears to be that the way to protect one's own satellites is to destroy those of the other side. Some efforts are being made to make satellites less vulnerable to attack, but limitations as to weight and size and the difficulties of concealing satellites suggest that offensive ASAT is the more likely path. The similarity of ASAT technologies to technologies for defence against ballistic missile attack suggest that progress in the former will continue to revive interest in the latter, despite the limitations on deployment of anit-ballistic missiles agreed between the USA and USSR.

Finally, it is clear that command, control, communications and intelligence are the weakest link in the counterforce chain, especially because of their vulnerability. The USA is attempting to improve the endurance and survivability of its C^3I despite the immense difficulties. For some elements of the C^3I capability, it is difficult to provide back-up systems; others cannot be made mobile, and others cannot be camouflaged because of their electronic emissions. But the whole history of nuclear strategy and the strength of the lure of counterforce should at least demonstrate one thing: even if a particular goal is hard to approach or impossible to attain, and even if attaining it would be futile, this does not mean the effort will not be made.

DETERRENCE, COUNTERFORCE AND DISARMAMENT

It is, of course, possible that the 1980s will not show the same course of technological development as the 1970s did. It is possible that different choices will be made, and a different path will be followed. If the possibility of choice is to exist, it will be because the politics and institutions of the armament process are subjected to a sharp, massive and sustained challenge. Essentially, the choice is between three different positions about nuclear weapons—one arguing for pure deterrence, one arguing for counterforce, and one arguing for disarmament.

It is clear from our arguments above that a strategy of pure nuclear deterrence is desperately flawed. It has too many unattractive aspects for political leaders, the military and civilians alike. It is effectively dysfunctional for the pursuit of the political interests it is established to protect. The flaws in pure deterrence suggest that to the extent that it is necessary it is inherently unstable and, conversely, to the extent that it is stable it is probably unnecessary. It suffers from the paradox of declaring nuclear weapons to be un-useable while demanding massive resources for their development and sophistication. It is constantly weakened by the very process of technological development it sets in motion, and this process weakens it further by tempting decision-makers into counterforce strategies which reassert the utility of nuclear weapons.

Yet the flaws of counterforce strategy are even greater than the flaws of pure deterrence. Even if the claim is made that counterforce strengthens deterrence, and even if this is genuinely believed by the military and political decision-makers, the effect of counterforce is to weaken deterrence at exactly the times when it should be strongest, at times of crisis. All the intricate theorising about the possibility of

30

rational use of nuclear weapons cannot remove the dangers and flaws of counterforce. Even if the declared strategy does not actively contemplate a disarming first strike, the deterioration of a political crisis to the point where war is looming could make it seem that the only 'rational' action is to strike first, throwing all theories of limited nuclear war out the window in the process. It is not the logical rigour of theories of limited nuclear war and the utility of nuclear weapons which is the problem: what is worrying is the apparent absorption and even obsession with such theories, despite their evident illogicality.

At one level it can be argued that this is the result of technological momentum which is essentially non-rational, which derives not from any strategic logic but from the technical possibilities available at any given time, from the power of institutions promoting and profiting from the technology, and from the dazzling effect of shiny new gadgetry on political decision-makers. Yet it is also true that the quest for doctrines asserting the utility of nuclear weapons is linked to the political and strategic assumption that military power is essential to the pursuit of the interests of the nation-state. Nuclear weapons are seen as indispensable and central components of military power—one could say, they have to be seen that way by the states which deploy them—and it is therefore axiomatic that they be useable components. Technological developments can seem to have such a powerful influence on strategy because they appear to provide solutions to problems which deeply concern decision-makers.

What is particularly worrying at the present time is the connection between these assumptions and the re-emerged assertion that the confrontation between the USA and the USSR is fundamental and essentially irreducible for the foreseeable future. Increasing multipolarity in world affairs has consistently eroded the credibility of this view. Yet it is precisely this view that lies at the heart of the Reagan administration's international perspectives. There is every sign of that administration wanting to cut through the tangled undergrowth of world politics as if everything could be reduced to the US-Soviet dimension. In so doing, it will

31

cause a great deal of damage and, because it is not attacking the objective it thinks it is, it will not improve what it appears to see as a weak American position. Along that path lie continuing frustrations in world affairs and ever-renewed bouts of hysteria. With the administration also wanting to make nuclear weapons into useable instruments of a misguided policy, the result could be tilting at windmills in an increasingly dangerous fashion.

Thus consideration of the immediate situation and of the fundamental flaws of counterforce make it essential that a decisive turn away from counterforce is made. Yet the instabilities of pure deterrence cannot be just wished away. A 'return' to pure deterrence cannot be contemplated: to attempt it would be, if our arguments are correct, merely to establish the process which would lead strategy back into counterforce within a relatively short period.

Two things follow. Firstly, it is clear that genuine reductions of nuclear forces require not only turning aside from counterforce but also rejecting the concept of stable nuclear deterrence. The alternative is to establish the pragmatic as well as the moral basis for nuclear disarmament. Secondly, it is also clear that it is possible to do just that— to advance pragmatic as well as moral arguments for nuclear disarmament and, indeed, to tie the two strands inextricably together. The dangers of counterforce bring home the impossibility of relying on nuclear deterrence, and therefore emphasise the need for nuclear disarmament. The increasing political breadth of concern about nuclear weapons in western Europe, focussing in the first place on the decision to deploy Pershing II and cruise missiles, is evidence for that assertion.

This provides us with a rather optimistic conclusion to an essay which has otherwise been necessarily grim. It may be that our optimism will be criticised on the grounds that our argument in this concluding section has relied heavily on rationality, a reliance which can be irrelevant in a world where irrational fears, distrusts and fantasies of power are easily exploited by massively powerful institutions whose own rationality relates only to short- and medium-term goals, not to long-term outcomes. This is not an easy criticism to answer. But it cannot be allowed to discourage those who wish to prevent nuclear war. While it is a truism that nobody wants a nuclear war, this has not prevented the military, political and technological establishments of the great powers (and some lesser ones) from preparing for it. If the truism is true, it seems the main tasks of those who wish to prevent nuclear war are to understand what forces are operating to make such a war more likely and to show that rational and logical alternatives exist. In the last analysis, we can only rely on human rationality to draw the correct conclusions.

NOTES

1. J.F. Dulles, speaking before the Council on Foreign Relations, 12 January 1954, reprinted in R.G. Head and E.J. Rokke, eds., *American Defense Policy* (Johns Hopkins University Press, Baltimore, 1973).
2. G.M. Malenkov, Chairman of the Council of Ministers of the USSR, speaking on 27 April 1954, quoted in H. Dinnerstein, *War and the Soviet Union* (Praeger, New York, 1962), p. 74.
3. K.S. Gray and K. Paine, 'Victory is Possible', *Foreign Policy*, no. 39, summer 1980.
4. T. Schelling, *Arms and Influence* (Yale University Press, New Haven, 1966), p. 10.
5. See A.C. Enthoven and K.W. Smith, *How Much is Enough? Shaping the Defense Program 1961-1969* (Harper & Row, New York, 1971).
6. See *US Department of State Bulletin*, 9 July 1962; also W.W. Kaufmann, *The McNamara Strategy* (Harper & Row, New York, 1964), p. 26.
7. See H. Brown, *Department of Defense Annual Report Fiscal Year 1982*, pp. 38-43.
8. See H. Dinnerstein, *War and the Soviet Union*, ch. 3; also *World Armaments & Disarmament: SIPRI Yearbook 1974* MIT Press, London, 1974), ch. 5.
9. *World Armament & Disarmament: SIPRI Yearbook 1975* (Almqvist & Wiksell, Stockholm, 1975), p. 44.
10. See Harold Brown's posture statement for FY 1982 (cited above, n7) and also for FY 1981; for a discussion of the tension within Brown's views, see E. Rothschild, 'The American Arms Boom', in E.P. Thompson and D. Smith, eds., *Protest and Survive* (Penguin, Harmondsworth, 1980).
11. B.S. Lambeth, 'Selective nuclear operations and Soviet strategy', in J.H. Holst and U. Nerlich, eds., *Beyond Nuclear Deterrence: New Aims, New Arms* (Macdonald & Jane's, London, 1977), pp. 80 & 87.
12. H.S. Rowen and A. Wohlstetter, 'Varying response with circumstances', in Holst & Nerlich, eds., *Beyond Nuclear Deterrence*, pp. 226-7.
13. Figures are taken from *World Armaments & Disarmament: SIPRI Yearbook 1981* (Taylor & Francis, London, 1981); the difference between the number of warheads required by each side in a theoretical first strike results from the different make-up of the two forces, with the USA having a much larger number of warheads based in missile-firing submarines; calculations based on the figures are further complicated by the presence

33

of US nuclear warheads in Europe which are not included here.

14. L.H. Gelb and R.K. Betts, *The Irony of Vietnam: The System Worked* (Brookings Institute, Washington, DC, 1979), p. 111.

15. W. Pincus in *International Herald Tribune*, 4 December 1978.

16. A. Cockburn and A. Cockburn, 'The Myth of missile accuracy', *New York Review of Books*, 20 November 1980.

17. For a more detailed review, see *SIPRI Yearbook 1981*, ch. 2.

18. *World Armaments & Disarmament: SIPRI Yearbook 1972* (Almqvist & Wiksell, Stockholm, 1972), p. 10.

19. *World Armaments & Disarmament: SIPRI Yearbook 1979* (Taylor & Francis, London, 1979), p. 12.

20. *The Military Balance 1980-1981* (International Institute for Strategic Studies, London, 1980), p. 89.

21. *World Armaments & Disarmament: SIPRI Yearbook 1969/70* (Almqvist & Wiksell, Stockholm, 1970), p. 56.

22. *Evaluation of Fiscal Year 1979 Arms Control Impact Statements*, Report prepared for the Subcommittee on International Security Scientific Affairs of the Committee on International Relations, US House of Representatives (US Government Printing Office, 1978), pp. 109-10.

23. *SIPRI Yearbook 1979*, p. 432.

24. A.G. Cameron, 'Spread spectrum technology effecting military communication', *Naval Research Reviews*, vol. 30, no. 9, spring 1977.

25. General G.S. Brown, *United States Military Force Posture for FY 1979*, p. 23.

26. *Authorization for Military Procurement Research and Development, FY 1970, and Reserve Strength*, Hearings before the Committee on Armed Services, US Senate (US Government Printing Office, 19 March 1969), p. 37.

27. *World Armaments & Disarmament: SIPRI Yearbook 1978* (Taylor & Francis, London, 1978), p. 127.

28. See Stockholm International Peace Research Institute, *Outer Space—Battlefield of the Future?* (Taylor & Francis, London, 1978), ch. 8.

29. C.A. Robinson, 'Ballistic missile defence emphasis urged', *Aviation Week & Space Technology*, 13 October 1980.

30. W. Pincus in *Washington Post*, 26 June 1980.

31. C. Paine, 'Pershing II: the Army's strategic weapon', *Bulletin of the Atomic Scientists*, vol. 36, no. 8, October 1980.

32. *SIPRI Yearbook 1978*, p. 453.

33. C.A. Robinson, 'Soviets testing new generation of ICBM's', *Aviation Week & Space Technology*, 3 November 1980.

NUCLEAR WEAPONS IN EUROPE

William Arkin

Modern military strategy and concepts of defence are becoming more and more dependent on the use of nuclear weapons. This is not simply because of NATO's alleged conventional inferiority. The fact is that neither side—NATO or the Warsaw Pact—would be likely to carry out any conceivable military operation against the other without resorting to nuclear weapons. Ample evidence is available to show that nuclear weapons are integral to East and West military formations and strategy and that their role in battlefield plans is becoming more important. Additional refinements to nuclear warfighting capacities go far beyond the known deterrence strategies associated with long-range nuclear systems.

Where is this leading us? If there is *ever* a war in Europe it will undoubtedly be a nuclear war. The number and diversity of weapons will lead to nuclear war not because of imbalances, or because of ambiguous distinctions between 'tactical', 'theatre', 'Eurostrategic' or 'strategic' weapons. The weapons will lead to a nuclear war because they are there. They are designed both for nuclear offence and nuclear defence; they are targeted on military and civilian installations; and they are kept in a hair-trigger configuration so as to preserve the illusion that nuclear victory is possible.

Four nations—Britain, France, the Soviet Union and the United States—have substantial nuclear weapons stockpiles, intended for nuclear warfare in Europe. Altogether there are over 15,000 warheads allocated directly for European contingencies and there are many more deployed in the United States and the Soviet Union which are available for Europe. The types of weapons vary tremendously: they range from short-range sub kiloton mines to intercontinental missiles with the explosive yield of over a million tons of TNT. There are over seventy different delivery systems. They are widely dispersed throughout the European land mass and the neighbouring oceans. In assessing nuclear capabilities, we also need to take into account the extensive infrastructure and reinforcements maintained in readiness for nuclear war.

Nuclear contingencies no longer have any logic to anyone other than the military. It is because of that that the prospects for reducing nuclear arsenals in Europe have never been better. When the facts are known, the case for a nuclear free Europe is obvious and urgent. This chapter describes the facts: the weapons, their characteristics, and how they would be used in a nuclear war.

The United States has the most extensive theatre nuclear capability. It spends about $2 billion a year on theatre nuclear forces[1] and has some 25,000 personnel assigned to nuclear duties in Europe. There are 722 nuclear certified units in the US military,[2] including naval ships, and a substantial European nuclear infrastructure. The US also supplies seven NATO nations with nuclear weapons for their delivery systems and some 100 allied units are certified as nuclear capable. This arrangement allows for the peacetime deployment of US nuclear weapons in Belgium, Italy, Greece, the Netherlands. Turkey, the United Kingdom and West Germany. Nuclear-equipped naval forces also call at other nations' ports and bases and nuclear capable aircraft utilise numerous airbases.

Besides the 7,000 warheads which the US maintains in Europe a further 10,000 tactical warheads could easily be transported to Europe. For instance, the US Air Force plans to triple its number of aircraft in Europe in the first seven days of a conflict, dispersing nuclear capable aircraft to seventy-three allied 'collocated operating bases'.

The US nuclear capability includes both tactical nuclear weapons designed for ground warfare and intercontinental strategic weapons which threaten Warsaw Pact cities and military bases. Within the Army, Navy and Air Force there is virtually no combat unit which is not equipped with nuclear weapons. The military staff is convinced that it could not defend Europe without its nuclear weapons and many nuclear weapons are kept on alert to respond quickly in case of crisis.

Research and development of new nuclear capabilities is a continuous process within the Department of Defense. There are over twenty different new weapons under development or study which will have relevance to nuclear warfare in Europe in the coming years. There is no indication that any real effort is being made to develop new conventional technologies which could replace obsolete and ineffective nuclear weapons in the future. In fact, nuclear weapons research continues to identify new technical possibilities for refining the ability to fight a nuclear war in Europe.

Britain is the only other state which both commits forces to NATO's integrated command system and has independent nuclear weapons. These weapons include Polaris submarine-launched ballistic missiles, nuclear bombs for British-designed aircraft and nuclear depth charges for anti-submarine warfare helicopters. The British armed forces are also equipped with American weapons which are controlled by the US military in Britain and West Germany—Lance missiles, nuclear artillery and nuclear depth bombs for anti-submarine warfare aircraft.

The future of Britain's 'independent' nuclear capability is hotly debated. Many different alternatives are being considered for the next generation of nuclear weapons. Some programmes are already underway and a commitment has been made to others (e.g. Trident, and Tornado). But their future remains uncertain. Whatever Britain decides, it will require close collaboration with the US in design, development, production and support.

France also maintains its own national nuclear force, completely outside NATO and developed without the aid of the USA. Its weapons include a variety of systems, from short-range to intermediate-range, land-based and submarine-based missiles. French nuclear forces are all deployed in France, except for its submarine force which patrols in the North Atlantic and its limited naval carrier force. France has built some 350 nuclear warheads since 1966 and is engaged in an ambitious and expensive modernisation programme. Its research and development programme includes a wide variety of very new weapons; many are scheduled for deployment in the late 1980s and 1990s.

The Soviet Union has an extensive European theatre nuclear capability but it is by no means superior to the combined NATO strength. The Soviet armed forces appear to have many more nuclear capable delivery systems deployed with its forces than nuclear warheads. It is reported that its tactical nuclear capability for Europe numbers anywhere from 3,500-6,000 nuclear weapons. The Department of Defense, however, has reported that it is not clear whether the nuclear warheads for those delivery systems in non-Soviet Eastern Europe are actually deployed.[3] The uncertainties about the storage and deployment patterns of Soviet nuclear weapons can be explained in a number of ways. First, as Secretary of Defense, Weinberger stressed in his press conference on the neutron bomb in August 1981, weapons can be quickly ('in a few hours') sent to Europe *from the United States* to be fitted to delivery systems. The ability of the Soviet Union to deploy nuclear weapons forward to its delivery systems is probably more than adequate. Second, the Soviet Union has much stricter security regulations than NATO. In a military system where even maps are classified, the security accorded nuclear weapons is paramount. According to accounts which have appeared in the open literature, special KGB troops guard nuclear weapons which are reportedly kept in 'safe' central depots. Finally, Soviet force structure is also quite different from NATO's. Even though the Soviet Union keeps a large force deployed in Eastern Europe, the armies, divisions and tactical air forces deployed there with FROG and SCUD missiles and nuclear capable aircraft do not represent the major element of Soviet theatre nuclear capabilities. Soviet nuclear forces for war in Europe consist mostly of missiles and bombers which are located in the Soviet Union.

Soviet theatre nuclear forces are generally divided into three geographic groups: those in Western USSR (Baltic, Carpathian and Byelorussian military districts) directed against Europe, those in the Soviet Far East which are directed against Asia, and those in the central USSR which could be used in either direction. Most of the Soviet forces, particularly the new weapons, are mobile and could be quickly brought into a conflict in Europe or in Asia. In addition, many strategic weapons in the Soviet inventory are apparently linked to theatre tasks, particularly the SS-11 and SS-19 intercontinental ballistic missiles.[4] Some recent reports have even spoken of mobile land versions of the naval SS-N-3 and SS-N-12 cruise missiles.[5]

SHORT-RANGE NUCLEAR WEAPONS *(See table)*

Often called battlefield weapons, short-range nuclear weapons are those which have a range of up to 200 kilometres. These are the most numerous types in the NATO inventory; the least numerous in the Warsaw Pact's. They include artillery, some surface-to-surface missiles, atomic demolition munitions (nuclear land mines), and surface-to-air missiles. Nuclear armed aircraft can also be used at short ranges, but no aircraft can be restrained to operate only within 200 kilometres. Short-range weapons are 'tactical' in that they are for use in non-preplanned strikes, mostly against non-fixed targets, to support or repel military attacks. According to the Department of Defense, short-range weapons 'achieve a quick, decisive reversal of the tactical situation'.[6]

Artillery

One third to one half of NATO's present inventory of 7,000 nuclear weapons in Europe are nuclear artillery projectiles. According to the Joint Chiefs of Staff, the Warsaw Pact is faced with 'possible nuclear capability in every artillery position across the entire front'.[7] Two calibres of nuclear projectiles exist in the NATO arsenal: 155 mm and 203 mm. There are presently eight types of nuclear capable 155 mm artillery guns and three types of nuclear capable 203 mm artillery guns in NATO. The two most prevalent non-nuclear capable artillery guns—105 mm and 175 mm—are being phased out in favour of 155 mm and 203 mm weapons. This will result in the addition of new nuclear capable units to NATO and increased requirements for nuclear projectiles. Nuclear projectiles are stockpiled for all of the NATO nations which have a nuclear capability. France does not have a nuclear capability in its artillery and is not known to be developing one.

The United States has thirty-five artillery battalions in Europe, all in West Germany, all with 155 mm and 203 mm guns, all nuclear certified and equipped. An artillery upgrade programme from 1976 to 1983 will result in the replacement of the non-nuclear 175 mm guns with the newest long-range versions of nuclear capable guns and will increase battalion size by adding six guns to each unit.

Two new nuclear shells are going to replace the current projectiles in the 1980s. The new 203 mm projectile entered production in July 1981 and will be modified as an enhanced radiation ('neutron bomb') weapon. The August 1981 decision to modify this warhead as well as new versions of the Lance warhead also included a decision not to deploy these new weapons to Europe for the time being. The new 203 mm neutron warhead has an estimated yield of one kiloton (compared to a ten kiloton yield of the current shell) and 800 are reportedly being produced. The new 155 mm nuclear shell is still in development and production will begin in 1983.

Ironically, while the military has lauded the capability of the neutron warhead to justify the production of the new 203 shell, no plans exist to produce the new 155 mm projectile as a neutron warhead.[8] Most division and brigade level artillery units in NATO have 155 mm guns and the new nuclear shells will be extensively deployed for them. Both of the new weapons have greater range than their predecessors (over twenty kilometres) and will be easier to fire and use.

Although credited for many years with a nuclear capability, Soviet and Warsaw Pact artillery is for the most part still conventional. The Department of Defense has stated that 203 mm and 240 mm artillery deployed in the Soviet Union have been adapted to fire nuclear projectiles and that the rounds have been produced for them.[9] These are not standard guns nor are they widely deployed. Nevertheless, development of new self-propelled 203 mm and 240 mm nuclear artillery guns has also begun.

The standard artillery guns within the Soviet Army— 122 mm, 130 mm, and 152 mm—are non-nuclear. The newest generation of Soviet artillery—self-propelled 122 mm and 152 mm guns—now being widely deployed in Eastern Europe have no nuclear capability. Although some sources have credited the Soviet Army with as many as 150 dual capable artillery tubes, nuclear artillery does not appear to play an important role in Soviet nuclear strategy. None of the other Warsaw Pact armies is known to have any nuclear capable artillery.

Surface-to-Surface missiles

NATO has two short-range nuclear capable missiles: Lance and Honest John. These 40-110 kilometre range weapons are used for 'general support' of military operations and are mostly under the control of Corps level commanders. Short-range missiles are not normally targeted on fixed installations but are mainly allocated for attacks on mobile command posts and headquarters, ammunition supply points in the field, and assembly areas. It is estimated that some 500 nuclear warheads for the Lance and Honest John missiles are stockpiled in Europe, including reloads. Their explosive yield varies from one to 100 kilotons. Greece and Turkey are the only NATO countries still using the older Honest John.

A follow on to the Lance, the 'Nuclear Corps Support Missile' (sometimes called the 'Corps Support Weapons System') is also being developed by the United States. It will improve accuracy over the present missiles, have a higher rate of fire, and a longer range. It is expected for deployment in the early 1990s.

France also has short-range Pluton missiles in its Army as part of its independent nuclear force. Five regiments with thirty launchers are deployed in France and could be used to support the three French divisions deployed in West Germany. Being studied as a replacement for the Pluton is the Hades/Super Pluton which would more than double the present range, and could be fitted with a neutron warhead also under development in France.

The Warsaw Pact places greater reliance on surface-to-surface missiles than NATO; this may account for their lack of nuclear artillery. The usual Soviet division includes nuclear capable FROG missiles (mostly the truck-mounted FROG-7 model) and four launchers are assigned to every division that is deployed forward, and every division in the Category I state of readiness (i.e. those divisions that are fully manned and equipped), as well as every mechanised and armoured division of the Warsaw Pact armies. The FROG missile is the only nuclear system in the Soviet division, compared with atomic demolition munitions, nuclear artillery and short-range missiles in NATO divisions. Nuclear warheads for the FROG are not kept at the division level, but are controlled higher up in the command hierarchy at the Army level. Only the Soviet and East German Armies appear to have nuclear warheads storage sites.

The low yield FROG warhead is intended to be used for general support of division operations, to destroy command posts and headquarters, fixed defence, and battlefield formations and strong points. A replacement missile, the SS-21, with greater range and improved accuracy was introduced into the Soviet military in 1979, but has not yet been deployed with forces outside the Soviet Union. Most Soviet and Warsaw Pact FROG units frequently practise procedures for nuclear missions. There is no evidence, however, that any sort of nuclear weapons custodial relationship exists at unit level between Soviet and other Warsaw Pact units as it does for US and allied forces.

Atomic demolition munitions

Some 300 nuclear land mines are stockpiled in Europe for use by US and NATO engineer and unconventional 'special forces' (commando) units. These include two types of ADMs, a large general purpose munition (medium ADM) and a small portable mine (special ADM) which range in explosive yield from .01 to one kiloton. ADMs are emplaced in chambers in the ground or on bridges, tunnels and dams, and are detonated by timer or remote command. They are used primarily to disrupt the movement of enemy forces and to make them concentrate in a mass to bypass obstacles (and thus create other targets for nuclear weapons). US Army 'special forces' have the secret mission of placing special ADMs behind enemy lines, particularly at airfields, command posts, transportation, communications and industrial terminals, and petroleum supplies. US Army units in West Germany and Italy, and a number of trained NATO engineer units have ADM missions. There does not appear to be a serious replacement for the ADMs now being considered by the Defense Department, and the Secretary of Defense has stated that ADMs 'will be reduced gradually as improved conventional systems are deployed'.[10] The Warsaw Pact does not have any atomic demolition munitions and is not known to be developing them.

Surface-to-Air missiles

Six NATO nations have some 600 nuclear warheads for high altitude Nike-Hercules surface-to-air missiles. The one kiloton weapon is intended to destroy massed Warsaw Pact air strikes, particularly large-scale bombing missions. The missiles can also be used for nuclear strikes on the ground up to sixty kilometres, but are very inaccurate. They are obsolescent and ineffective and are being reduced and phased out. A number of NATO batteries are already converted to conventional-only missions pending the introduction of the US Patriot surface-to-air-missile. All of the Nike-Hercules will be replaced by either the conventional Patriot or the Improved Hawk. The Patriot is planned for deployment to Europe in 1983. Indications are that the Army will be looking at a nuclear replacement for Nike Hercules in the future.[11]

Two battlefield surface-to-air missiles of the Warsaw Pact—SA-3 and SA-2—are credited by some analysts with a nuclear capability but the US Defense Department has never publicly reported their deployment with nuclear weapons.

MEDIUM- AND LONG-RANGE WEAPONS *(See table)*

In contrast to short-range battlefield weapons, medium- and long-range nuclear weapons[12] are intended for attacks on targets deep in the rear area of military formations or enemy territory. Long-range weapons are largely allocated for pre-planned strikes on strategic military and civilian targets. The immediate tactical significance of nuclear strikes of this sort is not known; they would not necessarily directly affect combat at the front lines. Two quite different arguments are put forward to justify their military utility; one, that nuclear strikes threatening destruction of important civilian, industrial and economic targets would cause a reassessment of continued military aggression or defence; and two, that in a prolonged war, numerous nuclear strikes deep in enemy territory directed at primarily military targets would eventually disrupt command, control, resupply and reinforcement and military operations at the front would falter.

Medium- and long-range weapons in Europe include tactical aircraft and medium bombers, ground-launched ballistic missiles of various ranges and submarine-launched ballistic missiles. Additional 'strategic' nuclear weapons deployed in the United States and the Soviet homeland could be used for nuclear war in Europe and would most likely be targeted against fixed hardened installations.

Tactical aircraft
Nuclear capable aircraft are the most common carriers of medium- and long-range weapons. Nuclear bombs are extremely accurate and tactical nuclear aircraft are very versatile. Their drawback is that they are dependent on vulnerable air bases, require sophisticated information systems to locate proper targets and can be destroyed on the way to their targets.

Theoretically every tactical fighter aircraft is nuclear capable, but only certain models, depending on their role in warfare, are 'nuclear certified' and assigned nuclear missions. The types of missions vary greatly, as do the capabilities of the aircraft. Nuclear-equipped units and wings are numerous and easily identifiable through reconnaissance of security measures at the weapons storage areas. NATO maintains certain aircraft loaded with nuclear bombs and on alert at about ten airfields; it does not appear that the Soviet Union has any aircraft on nuclear alert.

Nuclear-equipped aircraft carrying nuclear bombs can be allocated to the ground commander for direct tactical support and used for short-range missions. More commonly they are intended for preplanned attacks on specific strategic targets. It has been NATO practice to designate certain dual capable aircraft from fighter wings for specific nuclear missions; the

44

Warsaw Pact appears to retain its nuclear capability in the Soviet Union in bomber units and fighter wings which have general responsibilities. As the new long-range ground-launched cruise missiles (GLCM) and Pershing II systems are introduced into the NATO inventory, dual capable aircraft allocated to nuclear strike missions will be reduced.[13]

NATO has fourteen different aircraft types which are nuclear certified and eight countries have (or are supplied with) nuclear bombs for them. These aircraft can drop bombs ranging in yield from one kiloton (perhaps even less) to over one megaton, up to ranges of 3,000 kilometres. Of the NATO countries, the US maintains the largest tactical nuclear aircraft inventory, followed by Britain and West Germany and Turkey. US F-111 and A-6 aircraft (along with the older British Vulcan bombers) are particularly suited for long-range strike missions. From their bases in Britain and abroad aircraft carriers in the Mediterranean, they can hit targets well into the Soviet Union. Their characteristics for long-range missions include aerial refuelling, electronic counter-measures and penetration at low altitudes to evade enemy air defences. Other aircraft, like the F-4 or the British-French Jaguar are more suited to medium-range and battle-field support roles. For this mission, they are supplied with a low yield nuclear bomb. At medium ranges, these aircraft are assigned missions against mobile targets and command posts, supply centres and troop concentrations. Other carrier-based and reinforcing American aircraft are also assigned nuclear missions including short-range and long-range strikes.

The US has a wide variety of new nuclear capable aircraft in development or now entering the armed forces. The dual capability of these aircraft is enhanced, according to Department of Defense, by 'improved system penetration ability, responsiveness, survivability, and the continued replacement of older technology nuclear bombs with modern B-61 bombs'.[14] The most common new aircraft, the F-16, has been adopted by the Netherlands and Belgium in the nuclear role. It is also a possible contender for replacement of the ageing nuclear strike aircraft in the Greek and Turkish armed forces. The F-16 will begin to equip the first US fighter wing in West Germany in 1983, and is already in service with Belgian and Dutch Air Force units.

The Marine/Navy F-18 will begin deployment in 1982 and will eventually replace nuclear capable versions of the A-7 and A-4 and the non-nuclear capable Marine F-4.[15] Along with the new vertical take off and landing (V/STOL) AV-8B, which is nuclear capable, the Marine Corps will have two new nuclear capable aircraft. The Strike Eagle, another aircraft under development, would improve the present F-15 fighter for nuclear and attack missions. Under development since 1977, the new aircraft would have greatly increased payload and radius, be capable of operations at night and in all weather, and have radar and avionics capable of attacking pinpoint military targets.

Britain's independent nuclear capabilities include British designed and manufactured nuclear capable aircraft and nuclear bombs. These aircraft—Vulcan, Buccaneer and Jaguar (coproduced with France)—are committed to NATO and some are forward deployed in West Germany with the Royal Air Force.

A number of European nations are working on two new nuclear capable aircraft which will replace their current generation. The Tornado (a joint British, Italian and West German project) will begin to replace the Vulcan bomber in the British Air Force and older F-104 strike aircraft in the German and Italian Air Forces in 1981–82. Its all weather, low-level penetration and long-range strike radius makes it a significant improvement over the present nuclear strike aircraft. The introduction of the Tornado will double the inventory. Another nuclear capable aircraft in the design stage is the multinational European Combat Aircraft which would replace the current force of medium attack and fighter attack in the 1990s.

France also possesses an extensive national nuclear capability in tactical aircraft, divided between a long-range strategic force and a shorter-range tactical force. Over 100 nuclear capable aircraft—including Mirage IVAs, Mirage IIIEs, and Jaguars—are assigned to nuclear attack missions. In addition, the French also have two aircraft carriers which have thirty-six Super Etendard nuclear strike aircraft armed with fifteen-kiloton bombs.

In the mid-1980s, three new nuclear capable French aircraft will enter service: The Mirage F1, Mirage 2000, and the Mirage 4000. Two hundred Mirage 2000s are intended to replace the present strategic force of Mirage IVAs, increasing that force five fold. A supersonic air-to-surface missile, the ASMP (similar to the US strategic Short-Range Attack Missile), is being developed for deployment on the Mirage 2000. The two other aircraft, the Mirage 4000 and Mirage F1 will also be used in the nuclear role; the Mirage F1 will fill the gap between the present aircraft and the 4000 will be a tactical nuclear strike aircraft.

The Warsaw Pact makes extensive use of nuclear capable aircraft and has recently introduced new models suited for offensive missions. These new aircraft seem to indicate a greater emphasis on less manoeuvreable air-to-surface capabilities than on air-superiority missions.[16] The Backfire bomber, one of these new planes, has received the most attention but other aircraft show major qualitative improvements over their predecessors and have nuclear capabilities.

The Soviet Union largely relies on medium bombers in its 'Long-Range Aviation' force (the Soviet bomber force), for long-range theatre strike missions. The Backfire fits this role, capable of strikes deep into Western Europe. Even though it is larger than the equivalent US aircraft, the F-111, it carries a smaller payload, and its ability to refuel in the air is questionable. The Backfire carries nuclear bombs and nuclear air-to-surface missiles, including the new AS-6 King-fish nuclear missile.

Like the other bombers in the Soviet inventory, the main targets of the Backfire force would be strategic, military, and civilian installations, particularly airfields, ports, transportation and communications hubs, military bases and industrial facilities. The use of the Backfire for long-range theatre missions, however, is limited because of Soviet inferiority in surveillance and target acquisition systems, particularly at long ranges. Its ability to hit mobile targets, or to evade mobile defence is very low. The Backfire is in production at a rate of about thirty per year, with about two thirds targeted on Europe: roughly 50 per cent of those are said to be nuclear strike versions.[17]

47

A number of different models of tactical aircraft are also suspected of having a nuclear capability and of having medium- and short-range nuclear missions. The primary aircraft for direct support of the ground forces and for second echelon strikes are the Fencer and Fitter. The Fencers are all deployed in the Soviet Union. According to the Department of Defense 'some versions' of the Fishbed and Flogger are also nuclear capable, having both an air combat and an air-to-surface role.[18] Some of the other older aircraft may also be nuclear capable but their range and accuracy, as well as their ability to penetrate, are very low. Combat performance of the latest model US aircraft—F-14, F-15, and F-16—is still superior to the latest generation of Soviet aircraft: Flogger, Fitter and Fencer.[19]

Little is known about the yields of Soviet nuclear bombs, or of the new air-to-surface missiles which have recently been introduced.

Although many counts of Warsaw Pact aircraft give figures for the number of medium bombers deployed throughout the Soviet Union with long-range aviation, the US Department of Defense reports forty of the sixty-five to seventy 'strike-configured' Backfires and 350 of 450 older bombers (Badger and Blinder) are in Europe or within striking distance of Europe.[20]

Ground-Based Missiles

Supplementing nuclear aircraft are medium- and long-range missiles which are targeted and intended for attacks against fixed military installations and certain strategic economic, communications and transportation points. Missiles are generally the most reliable (not defensible against) and survivable (if mobile) medium- and long-range weapons. Ballistic missiles have an extremely short flight time; some ten minutes to their maximum range. NATO has 180 Pershing I missiles in US and West German forces and France has eighteen intermediate-range ballistic missiles which are solely signed for nuclear strike missions. Some of the Pershing missiles are on alert for use against high priority targets, including enemy nuclear delivery systems. The Soviet inventory includes a number of ground-based missiles, a class of weapons on which they concentrate heavily. A high percentage of all of the ground-based missiles are located at known fixed sites and could be destroyed in a pre-emptive strike.

A replacement for the present US Pershing I missile, the Pershing II, is now finishing development in the US, and will be deployed starting in 1983 in West Germany. The new missile uses a guidance system which is the most accurate of any missile in the US and Soviet arsenal, including strategic missiles. Its range has increased two-and-a-half times to 1,800 kilometres making it the most effective counterforce weapon planned for Europe. It will be extremely effective and will be targeted on urgent hard targets including nuclear storage sites and delivery points, as well as command and control facilities. Its new warhead will have a low yield and will be capable of air or surface burst.[21] One hundred and eight launchers (with reload missiles) will be deployed with US forces in West Germany, from which they will have a very short (about five minutes) flight time to the Soviet Union. Like the ground-launched cruise missile, the Pershing II units will also be given a strategic mission and be directly tied into the command and control network for strategic nuclear forces. The US is also keeping open the option of developing a short-range version of the Pershing II for West German use and for other NATO purposes.[22]

Since 1971, France has had intermediate-range ballistic missiles deployed in semi-hardened silos in southeastern France. They are armed with a single megaton warhead and are superior to the equivalent Soviet missiles, the SS-4 and SS-5s, which are not deployed in solos and have less accuracy.

With the deployment in the Soviet Union of the counterforce capable SS-20, France is considering a mobile replacement for its present IRBMs in silos. This new missile, the SX, will carry between three and seven MIRV warheads and have a range of 2,000 miles.

The newest addition to the ground-based missile arsenal is the cruise missile. The ground-launched cruise missile (GLCM), under development by the United States since the early 1970s is planned for deployment to Europe starting in 1983. The missile has long-range capability (2,500 kilometres), a 200 kiloton warhead and super accuracy with its terrain-contour matching guidance. One hundred and sixteen launchers are planned for deployment in Italy, Belgium, West Germany, the Netherlands and Britain. Both Belgium and the Netherlands seem almost certain to reject their share of twenty-four launchers. GLCMs will be capable of hitting targets with great accuracy throughout Eastern Europe and in the Western Soviet Union. They are suited for destroying hard targets because of their accuracy, and would be targeted on command and control facilities, nuclear storage sites and delivery units, airfields, staging and assembly areas, and logistic facilities.[23] Their counterforce functions are limited by their slow flight time, taking about three hours of subsonic flight to go 1,500 miles. Their mobility and survivability make them suited for longer periods of warfare. Like the Pershing II, they will be tied directly into US strategic nuclear plans, via special communications transponders to satellites.

Another missile which has also been under consideration by the Department of Defense is the medium-range ballistic missile (codename Long Bow). Various studies have suggested a lightweight, high mobility, air- or ground-launched, quick reaction cruise ballistic missile, which has an initial ballistic trajectory but then converts to a cruise missile to penetrate air defences. Work on the missile has been done on and off since 1976, but full scale development funds have been denied in favour of Pershing II and GLCM.[24] The air launched Long Bow concept has been rejected in favour of the Advanced Strategic Air Launched Missile (ASALM), which would have the dual mission of shooting down Soviet radar-carrying aircraft and striking ground targets at ranges in excess of the existing Short-Range Attack Missiles.[25]

The central elements of the Warsaw Pact's theatre nuclear capability are its medium- and long-range missile forces, from the 300 km SCUD to the 5,000 km SS-20s. At the battlefield level, SCUD missiles are deployed with each Warsaw Pact army, throughout Eastern Europe. Only the SCUD missiles in the Soviet and East German armies appear to be supplied with nuclear warheads. SCUD missiles are mobile and provide general support to the front commander similar to the Pershing I. They are thought to be targeted on defensive, command and control, nuclear and logistic targets in the rear area.

The SS-12 Scaleboard, a longer range missile (range 800 kilometres), is also allocated for medium-range theatre missions. It has never been deployed outside the Soviet Union and its range would require deployment forward out of the USSR to strike targets throughout Europe. The replacements for both the SCUD and the SS-12 appear to have been developed and will be deployed in the coming years. The SS-22 replacement for the Scaleboard was first introduced in 1980, but has not yet been deployed in large numbers. The SS-X-23 replacement for the SCUD is in the development stage, and will probably be deployed in large numbers in the mid-1980s. Both of these missiles have better accuracy than their predecessors, but come nowhere near the accuracy of the newest generation of middle-range missiles under development in the US. These missiles will probably be extensively deployed, as they are the centre piece of Soviet tactical battlefield nuclear capabilities.

For long-range theatre nuclear warfare, older SS-4 and SS-5 missiles, and the newer SS-20s are stationed at sites throughout the Western USSR and are capable of hitting a wide assortment of targets in Western Europe. These weapons (except for the newer SS-20) along with the SCUD and Scaleboard missiles are not sufficiently accurate for striking small military targets. Since 1967, the SS-4s and SS-5s have been reduced from their highest deployment level of 750, to less than 400 today, with all of the remaining launchers targetable on Western Europe.[26]

The newest Soviet missile in the long-range theatre inventory is the SS-20, which has greater accuracy than earlier medium- and intermediate-range missiles, is mobile, and uses a lower yield MIRVed warhead. Initially, it was thought that the SS-20 would replace the older missiles on a one-for-one basis, but SS-4 and SS-5 withdrawals are not occurring at the anticipated rate.[27] The Department of Defence estimates (as of 1 January 1981) that 119 SS-20 launchers of 180 deployed throughout the Soviet Union are within striking distance of Europe. The SS-20s are deployed in three geographic areas, the Western USSR, central USSR, and the Soviet Far East at twenty-three sites.[28] The missile is in production at a rate of some fifty to 100 per year, and is being deployed at a constant rate of one per week.[29]

Initially deployed in 1977, the SS-20 represents the only long-range counterforce weapon solely designed for nuclear missions, which has assured penetration and sufficient accuracy to strike the full array of NATO and Western European targets. It has three warheads; all older Soviet weapons have one warhead.

Submarine-Launched Ballistic Missiles

All of the four nuclear weapon states have allocated submarine-launched nuclear missiles to the European theatre. Because they are difficult to detect by surveillance they are the most versatile medium- and long-range weapons that have been developed. The US commits 400 of its Poseidon warheads[30] and Britain commits 192 Polaris warheads to NATO's targets. France maintains an independent force of eighty missiles which are capable of striking throughout Eastern Europe and into the Soviet Union. The Soviet Union also allocates certain SLBMs to theatre nuclear warfare, and has some missiles which are unable to reach the US in its submarine force.

The accuracies of the theatre-allocated submarine missiles vary greatly. The newer Trident 1 and Poseidon have limited counterforce applications and can be used to attack a broad spectrum of military and civilian bases and installations. The older Polaris and Soviet missiles would not be very useful in a direct hit on small military targets, but their explosive yield would be capable of destroying any non-hardened installation. They are thought to be targeted on large complexes, ports and cities. The French missiles also have limited counterforce capabilities but are inferior to the Poseidon missiles. All of the Western submarine missiles can strike targets far into the Soviet Union. At any one time about five US, British and French submarines are on patrol for theatre missions. Soviet submarines generally stay closer to their home ports, and some would be limited to enclosed bodies of water in wartime (e.g. Black Sea, Baltic Sea).

The United States allocates a portion of its strategic missile force to the Supreme Allied Commander Europe (SACEUR) for 'general nuclear responses' and they are an important element of the NATO long-range category of weapons which are often overlooked. The British and French submarine forces are independent of US control, but also contribute to NATO theatre nuclear forces. The British forces are assigned to NATO but can be withdrawn for national need. The French forces are strictly independent but are clearly targeted against Warsaw Pact military and civilian targets.

Both Britain and France are embarking on modernisation and improvement plans which will greatly increase their capabilities. A manoeuvring re-entry vehicle with penetration aids (Chevaline) has been under development by Britain since 1969. It will improve the capabilities of the present Polaris missiles and could be used in future submarine forces. The French submarine construction programme will result in the completion of a sixth nuclear ballistic missile submarine in 1985. As many as eight submarines are possible by the early 1990s. In 1980 Britain announced its intention to replace the Polaris system with the American Trident missile and a new submarine. This could result in four or five new submarines in the 1990s which would eventually be deployed with the Trident II (D5) counterforce missile now in development in the US. The so-called 'modernisation' of the British and French submarine forces could result in a seven-fold increase in long-range warheads for these forces.

The older Soviet SLBM, the SS-N-5, is of limited range and poor accuracy. Since 1976, six Golf II ballistic missile submarines with eighteen SS-N-5s have been stationed in the Baltic and about five Hotel II ballistic missile submarines (also with the SS-N-5) are deployed with the Northern Fleet.[31] As newer Soviet submarines and missiles replace the older submarines in the Baltic and Northern fleets, they could be given European missions like the American Poseidons. For the time being, the older SS-N-5s are useful against large targets and cities; their one megaton warheads have the highest yield in the theatre nuclear forces.

NAVAL NUCLEAR WARFARE

A new and growing area of East-West competition is naval nuclear warfare. For many years, its future was questioned by weapons experts and strategists who regarded new conventional precision-guided naval weapons (missiles, torpedoes, guns etc.) as superior to the use of nuclear weapons at sea. In naval warfare, the use of nuclear weapons would have a particularly detrimental effect by destroying or degrading surveillance, acoustic, navigational/positional and communication systems essential for naval operations.

As the issue of theatre nuclear warfare has gained attention, the possibility of extending nuclear warfare to the seas has also been examined. From 1978 to 1980 a study by the Department of Defense and the Navy examined the utility of nuclear weapons in a war at sea.[32] Presumably because of the need to involve the Navy in the nuclear game, the study concluded that the Navy should continue to rely on nuclear weapons already deployed and should extend the role of nuclear weapons into other areas. This was justified primarily by the development and deployment of Soviet cruise missiles and the Backfire bomber. The Soviet Navy is also feared to have deployed a wide variety of other nuclear weapons, including 'naval torpedoes. . . depth bombers. . . fleet surface-to-air missiles. . . and naval artillery'.[33]

Many of the new American developments in the nuclear field are intended for long-range attack missions, but work is now also under way on new anti-submarine, anti-ship and anti-air nuclear weapons. Since 1974, the funds have been appropriated for the development of nuclear warheads for Harpoon, Standard and the Mark 46 torpedo. Production of the Harpoon and Standard nuclear warheads has also been authorised.

A large and growing area of naval nuclear warfare is anti-submarine warfare. The United States and Britain maintain a mammoth anti-submarine warfare capability which depends heavily on nuclear weapons.

Nuclear ASW systems are deployed aboard almost all US naval warships and submarines operating in the European area. Shipboard nuclear rocket torpedos (ASROC and SUBROC) equip cruisers, destroyers, frigates and submarines.

Nuclear depth bombs are deployed on aircraft carriers and ships which have ASW helicopter detachments. Long-range P13 Orion patrol aircraft operate regularly from numerous European airfields. Nuclear capable Terrier surface-to-air missiles are in service with a number of surface ships in the Navy.

Britain maintains four types of ASW helicopters (Sea King, Wessex, Wasp and Lynx) which are assigned to nuclear missions and equipped with British nuclear depth bombs. They operate from Royal Navy ships and from shore bases. Long-range ASW capability is provided by Nimrod patrol aircraft which are designed to carry US-made nuclear depth bombs (also carried on the US P-3s). The mission of these aircraft is to destroy submarines in the North Atlantic and the North Sea.

The US will soon begin widespread deployment of Tomahawk sea-launched cruise missiles (SLCMs), which will eventually become the most numerous nuclear weapon at sea. Over 3,000 SLCMs are planned by the US Navy for deployment on surface ships and submarines. The SLCM is similar to the ground-launched version but will be carried on submarines and ships and will have a dual capability for anti-ship and land attack warfare. Eventually, nuclear armed SLCMs could be deployed on aircraft operating from aircraft carriers in the European theatre.

During the 1978–79 period, the Soviet Union deployed submarines carrying nuclear-armed cruise missiles in the Baltic,[34] clearly directed against Europe. The Soviet Navy has deployed two nuclear cruise missiles: the SS-N-3 and the SS-N-12. Their continuing deployment on Echo and Juliet class submarines, as well as in newer submarines and surface ships, adds greatly to the medium attack capability of the Soviet Union. The Soviet SLCMs, however, are not as advanced as the US cruise missiles and in general the Soviet Union has a limited capacity for hitting targets beyond the horizon.

ANTI-TACTICAL MISSILES
The development of an anti-tactical ballistic missile (ATBM) capability is on the horizon for both the US and the Soviet Union. In the US, the concept is of a mini-ABM system to

protect American weapons from a first strike by the Soviet SS-20. According to Congressional testimony, the Soviet Union has embarked on an 'aggressive' ATBM programme.[35] It is thought to be driven by Soviet perceptions of the need to counter the super-accurate Pershing II.

In response to the possible development of a Soviet ATBM system, penetration aids are being developed in the Air Force Advanced Ballistic Reentry Systems (ABRES) programme for the Pershing II and other Army missile systems.[36] A joint Army/Air Force study is also assessing other methods of passive protection for the theatre nuclear forces (deception, camouflage, decoys, etc.).

The US ATBM programme represents a costly investment in a system designed to intercept Soviet missile warheads. According to reports, the system includes acquisition and tracking radars, signal processors, a high speed high accelera-tion missile, terminal homing, and a lethal interceptor war-head.[37] Many in the Department of Defense believe, however, that the cost of such a programme would be prohibitive compared with the addition of further mobile long-range theatre weapons like Pershing and SLCM. The need to deploy such a system will be considered greater if the Soviet Union appears to be making any progress in the ATBM area.

CONCLUSION

While the 'modernisation' of long-range theatre nuclear forces is largely dominated by discussions of the perceived changes in NATO and Warsaw Pact forces and the theoretical advan-tages accruing to each side, the continuous improvement and replacement of nuclear weapons clearly improves the offen-sive and warfighting capabilities of the ground, air and naval forces.

All of the new weapons for both NATO and the Warsaw Pact incorporate a number of 'improvements':

—increased range
—better accuracy
—improved survivability and mobility
—better command, control, and communications for a long war.

These have taken place in conjunction with other improvements: hardening of nuclear storage sites against attack, improved ability to identify small targets at long range, and lower collateral damage as a consequence of increased accuracy and lower or special (e.g. enhanced radiation) yields. The end result: a system in which nuclear weapons are integrated into every level of NATO's European war machine— in short, a system for nuclear war in Europe.

That war would destroy the very territory which the weapons are supposed to be protecting. The facts about the nuclear system are clear. The response should be to destroy the prospects for a nuclear war in Europe, before Europe is destroyed.

SHORT-RANGE NUCLEAR WEAPONS

	First Deployed	Range (km)	Nuclear Capable Launchers[1]	Yield (kt)	Countries
NATO/France					
155mm Artillery[2]	1964[3]	18	1690	Sub kt-2	Belgium, W. Germany, Greece, Italy, Netherlands, Turkey, UK, US
203mm Artillery[4]	1962[5]	17	390	Sub kt-10	Belgium, W. Germany, Greece, Netherlands, Turkey, UK, US
Honest John	1958	40	26	20	Greece, Turkey
Lance	1972	70-110	117	1-100	Belgium, W. Germany, Italy, Netherlands, UK, US
Pluton	1974	120	30	15-25	France
Atomic Demolition Munitions	1964	–	(300)	01-15	US
Nike Hercules	1958	140	748	1-20	Belgium, W. Germany, Greece, Italy, Netherlands, Turkey, US
Warsaw Pact					
203mm Artillery	–[7]	29	?	low kt	USSR
240mm Artillery	–[7]	10	?	low kt	USSR
FROG 3-7	1965	16-70	500	1-10	Bulgaria, Czechoslovakia, E. Germany, Hungary, Poland, Roumania, USSR
SS-21	1979	65-120	?	1	USSR

Notes next page

SHORT-RANGE NUCLEAR WEAPONS: Notes

1. Launchers (except for ADMs) include only those US and Soviet launchers in Europe or Western USSR.

2. Most common artillery piece is M-109, for which characteristics are given; other nuclear capable 155mm artillery pieces are FH-70, M-44, M-53, M-59, M-114, M-198 and SP-70.

3. IOC of M-109.

4. Most common artillery piece is M-110, for which characteristics are given; other nuclear capable 203mm artillery pieces are M-55 and M-115.

5. IOC of M-110.

6. Other NATO countries are trained to use ADMs.

7. The numbers and types are not clear; 180mm and 152mm are also claimed by some to be nuclear capable; Fiscal Year 1982, Joint Chiefs of Staff statement, US Military Posture, reports the 'introduction' of Soviet nuclear artillery.

MEDIUM- AND LONG-RANGE NUCLEAR WEAPONS

	First Deployed	Range (km)	Nuclear Capable Launchers[1]	Yield (kt)	Countries
NATO/France					
Medium-Range[2] aircraft	1954	—[3]	2023[4]	1-1000	Belgium, W. Germany, Greece, Italy, Netherlands, Turkey, UK, US, France
Long-Range[2] aircraft	1958[5]	—[6]	604[7]	1-1000	France, US, UK
MSBS M-20 SLBM[8]	1977	3,000	80	1.000	France
Pershing I	1962	160-720	180	60-400	W. Germany, US
Polaris SLBM	1967	4,600	64	3 x 200	UK
Poseidon SLBM[9]	1971	4,600	40-45[10]	9-10 x 50[11]	US
SSBS S-2 IRBM	1971	3,000	9	150	France
SSBS S-3 IRBM	1980	3.500	9	1000	France
Warsaw Pact					
Medium-Range[12] aircraft	1959	400-750	3300[13]	?	Czechoslovakia, Poland, USSR, E. Germany
Long-Range[14] aircraft	1955	1600-4000	888	?	USSR
SCUD[15]	1965	160-300	530[16]	low kt	Bulgaria, Czechoslovakia, E. Germany, Hungary, Poland, Roumania, USSR
SS-4	1959	1,900	350	1000	USSR
SS-5	1961	4,100	60	1000	USSR
SS-12	1969	490-900	120	1000	USSR
SS-20	1977	5,000	110	3 x 150	USSR
SS-22	1980	?	?	?	USSR
SS-N-5	1964	1,120	33	1000	USSR

Notes next page

NUCLEAR WEAPONS IN EUROPE

MEDIUM- AND LONG-RANGE NUCLEAR WEAPONS: Notes

1. Includes *all* nuclear capable launchers in Europe or committed to Europe in 1981. Not all nuclear capable launchers are supplied with nuclear warheads. Totals are included in order to arrive at equivalent estimates on both sides. Many Western estimates tend to give the total number of launchers on the Warsaw Pact side but only those known to be supplied with nuclear warheads on the Western side. The proportion of Warsaw Pact launchers supplied with nuclear warheads is not known.

2. Medium-range aircraft include A-4, A-7, Buccaneer, F-4, F-16, F-100, F-104, Jaguar, Mirage IIIE, Super Etendard, Tornado; long-range aircraft include A-6, F-111, Vulcan B2.

3. Combat radius of aircraft loaded with nuclear weapons without aerial refuelling varies from 400-1, 200 for NATO medium-range aircraft.

4. Includes aircraft in Europe, in countries with nuclear capabilities (excludes Canada, Denmark, Norway, Portugal, Luxembourg).

5. IOC of latest generation of long-range aircraft, US strategic bombers with ranges similar to today's long-range aircraft were stationed in Europe earlier.

6. Combat radius of aircraft loaded with nuclear weapons with aerial refuelling varies from 1,600-5,000.

7. Includes aircraft in Europe and US aircraft dual committed to NATO in the US (i.e. under the command of SACEUR).

8. Older M-2 missile being phased out in favour of M-20.

9. Newer Trident I missiles are also in Poseidon submarines and could be committed to NATO when those submarines deploy.

10. 400 warheads formally committed to NATO.

11. Yield of each MIRV.

12. Medium-range aircraft include Mig-21 Fishbed J/K/L/N, Mig-23/27 Flogger B/D, Su-7 Fitter A, SU-17 Fitter C/D; about 30 per cent of these fighters are deployed in Eastern Europe.

13. Number is total in Soviet Air Force and designated non-Soviet Warsaw Pact (excluding Roumania and Bulgaria).

14. Long-range aircraft include SU-19/24 Fencer, TU-16 Badger, TU-22 Blinder, TU-26 (TU-22M) Backfire.

15. Mostly SCUD B, still some SCUD A in non-Soviet forces.

16. Includes those which are thought nuclear capable.

DISARMING EUROPE

NOTES

1. US Congress, Senate, Committee on Armed Services, *Department of Defense Authorization for Appropriations for Fiscal Year 1981*, Hearings, 96th Congress, Second Session, Part 5, p. 2991. (Hereinafter referred to as 'SASC, DOD Auth, FY 1981. . .').
2. US Congress, Senate, Committee on Appropriations, *Department of Defense Appropriations, Fiscal Year 1981*, Hearings, 96th Congress, Second Session, Part 3, p. 730.
3. US Department of Defense, Secretary of Defense, *Department of Defense Annual Report, Fiscal Year 1979*, p. 69.
4. The SS-14 reported by some as an IRBM allocated to TNF was never deployed; Lawrence Freedman, 'The Dilemma of Theater Nuclear Arms Control', *Survival*, Jan/Feb 1981.
5. Stockholm International Peace Research Institute, *World Armaments and Disarmament, SIPRI Yearbook 1980*, (London: Taylor & Francis, Ltd, 1980), p. 177.
6. US Department of Defense, Secretary of Defense, *Department of Defense Annual Report, Fiscal Year 1976*, p. 111-3.
7. US Department of Defense, Joint Chiefs of Staff, *United States Military Posture for FY 1977*, p. 70.
8. The new 155mm projectile, the W82, is technically capable of accepting an enhanced radiation feature; US Department of Defense, Joint Chiefs of Staff, *United States Military Posture for Fiscal Year 1981*, p. 47.
9. SASC, DOD Auth, FY1981, Part 1, p. 364.
10. US Department of Defense, Secretary of Defense, *Department of Defense Annual Report, Fiscal Year 1982*, p. 128.
11. SASC, DOD Auth, FY 1981, Part 1, p. 393.
12. The medium (circa 200 km+) and long-range (circa 1,000 km+) designations are somewhat arbitrary, especially considering similarity in targets for some aircraft models.
13. *Department of Defense Annual Report, Fiscal Year 1982*, op. cit., p. 126.
14. *United States Military Posture for Fiscal Year 1980*, op. cit., p. 32.
15. The present Marine Corps F-4 and AV-8A are not nuclear-capable.
16. SASC, DOD Auth, FY 1981, Part 4, p. 1939.
17. *SIPRI Yearbook 1980*, op. cit., p. 180; SAC, DOD Approp, FY 1981, Part 5, p. 1630.
18. SASC, DOD Auth, FY 1981, Part 4, p. 1939.
19. Ibid.
20. *Department of Defense Annual Report, Fiscal Year 1982*, op. cit., p. 66.
21. The development of the 'earth penetration' warhead, another alternative for hitting bunkers and hardened facilities was terminated in January 1981; limited development continues and its future remains uncertain; US Department of Defense, *The Department of Defense Program for Research, Development and Acquisition*, Fiscal Year 1982, p. VII-8.
22. US Congress, House, Committee on Appropriations, *Department of Defense Appropriations, Fiscal Year 1981*, Hearings, 96th Congress, Second Session, Part 3, p. 691.
23. US Department of Defense, *The Fiscal Year 1980 Department of Defense Program for Research, Development and Acquisition*, p. VII-9.
24. SASC, DOD Auth, FY 1981, Part 5, p. 3013.
25. SASC, DOD Auth, FY 1981, Part 5, p. 3012.
26. Lawrence Freedman, op. cit.

27. Harold Brown, at Press Conference following Nuclear Planning Group Meeting in Bodo, Norway, 4 June 1980.
28. *Department of Defense Annual Report, Fiscal Year 1982,* p. 67; Lawrence Freedman, op. cit.
29. Directorate for Defense Information, Office of the Secretary of Defense (Public Affairs), US Department of Defense, Press Query from morning briefing, 12 February 1981.
30. Since late 1979, Trident missiles have begun equipping 12 Poseidon submarines and it is assumed that when on patrol, they could be committed to NATO, although no announcement has been made regarding the new missiles.
31. Raymond L. Garthoff, 'Brezhnev's Opening: The TNF Tangle', *Foreign Policy,* Number 41, Winter 1980–81.
32. SASC, DOD Auth, FY 1981, Part 5, p. 2990.
33. *The Department of Defense Program for Research, Development and Acquisition, Fiscal Year 1979,* p. IV-90; *The Department of Defense Program for Research, Development and Acquisition, Fiscal Year 1977,* p. IV-102.
34. Harold Brown at Press Conference following Nuclear Planning Group Meeting in Bodo, Norway, 4 June 1980.
35. SASC, DOD Auth, FY 1981, Part 5, p. 3013.
36. SASC, DOD Auth, FY 1981, Part 5, pp. 2827–2828.
37. SASC, DOD Auth, FY 1981, Part 5, p. 3014.

THEATRE NUCLEAR WEAPONS: THE NATO DOCTRINE

Sverre Lodgaard

European countries face hard decisions about Long-Range Theatre Nuclear Forces (LRTNFs). It is not just up to governments, in their usual exclusive style, to make these decisions. Public opinion—stronger and more encompassing than ever since the end of the Second World War—also has a say. It is precisely this that makes it so hard for the average politician and establishment expert who are used to making ad hoc decisions and muddling their way through. For the genuinely security-minded it offers a glimmer of hope. Public opinion is not looking for a workable compromise in order to dispose of the LRTNF issue. Public opinion is concerned with the substance of the issue and seeks a solution that will reduce the nuclear threat to Europe.

It would be most unfortunate if European governments became preoccupied with resisting and opposing these movements of public opinion. Instead they should seize the opportunity to reassess where we stand. They should approach the fundamental dilemmas of European security with the necessary vigour to reduce our predicament and they should give positive direction to public activity. Until recently European leaders lacked the public support to take such action even if they wanted to. They had no option but to live with the flaws and dilemmas. Today, the situation is radically different.

THE HISTORY OF LRTNFS
LRTNFs are nuclear weapons with a maximum range of more than 1,000 kilometres, intended for use in Europe or at least capable of being used against targets on European territory. As usual, the range specification is somewhat arbitrary, but

serves the purpose of focusing attention on a certain set of nuclear weapons systems. Nor is it easy to classify all systems according to this criterion: the Soviet SS-22 missile replacing the SS-12 Scaleboard has a range of about 1,000 kilometres—perhaps a little more or less—and a number of aircraft are extremely difficult to classify.

In the summer of 1949, the United States deployed 32 B-29 bombers to Britain. The B-29 'superfortress' has a radius of operation of about 2,500 kilometres, and therefore depended on forward bases for strikes against the Soviet Union. This was the beginning of the US Forward Based Systems (FBSs) in Europe.[1]

At this time, the B-52 was on the drawing boards. However, in order to acquire jet-bomber capability as soon as possible, priority was given to the Boeing B-47 medium-range bomber; the technological challenge was less than for an intercontinental aircraft, and the overseas bases were regarded as safe. The B-47 entered operational service in 1951, and remained the mainstay of Strategic Air Command (SAC) for 10 years. More than 2,000 were built, and the last ones were phased out in 1966. B-47s operated from bases in French Morocco, Spain and Britain, with units rotating from the USA.

Throughout the '50s, a variety of other nuclear capable aircraft (both land- and carrier-based) were also deployed to Europe and European waters, some of them capable of striking against the Soviet Union.[2]

The Karman Committee of 1945, which summarised the recent advances in science and technology, concluded that the US should concentrate on developing jet aircraft, whereas missiles belonged to a more distant future.[3] Nevertheless, the military services began small-scale missile programmes, often based on technology inherited from German wartime efforts. In the field of long-range vehicles, efforts were concentrated on aerodynamic, cruise missiles. The Navy operated its dual-purpose 650 kilometre range Regulus cruise missile on board submarines from 1954 to 1964. The Air Force missile programme was somewhat more ambitious, and more than 1,000 dual-capable (ie, able to carry nuclear or conventional warheads), supersonic Matador cruise missiles, with a range of about 800 kilometres, were produced. The Matador was placed with units in West Germany in the mid-'50s.[4] Some years later, it was replaced by another cruise missile, the Mace A/B, with a range of up to 2,500 kilometres. The Mace was withdrawn in the second half of the '60s for lack of manoeuverability and, subsequently, for its vulnerability to new generations of jet-propelled air-defence aircraft.[5]

At the NATO meeting in Washington in December, 1957, it was decided to deploy intermediate-range ballistic missiles (IRBMs) to Europe. In 1960, Thor and Jupiter missiles became operational in Britain, Italy and Turkey. They had a range of approximately 3,000 kilometres, and a warhead yield of 1.5 megatons. The 60 Thor missiles deployed to Britain were deactivated by the end of 1963, while the Jupiters (30 in Italy and 15 in Turkey) were phased out by 1965. The modest numbers and short lifetime were due to slow count-down, high vulnerability and, more important, the introduction of submarine-launched ballistic missiles (SLBMs) and land-based inter continental ballistic missiles (ICBMs). Polaris submarines were already patrolling the Mediterranean and the Norwegian sea when the first IRBMs were withdrawn.[6]

Soviet LRTNF deployments came largely in response to the US forward-based systems. Partly, they also compensated for the US lead in intercontinental weapons. While the Soviets waited for their own intercontinental missiles, Western Europe was held hostage. Finally, Soviet LRTNFs must be seen in relation to British and French nuclear forces capable of hitting Soviet territory.

Soviet LRTNFs reached a peak in the mid-'60s when altogether (including missiles targeted against China) 773 MRBMs/IRBMs were operational, and 880 medium-range bombers were available for strikes against Western Europe. The missiles were of three types: the 1,200 kilometre-range SS-3s (40 only), the 1,800 kilometre-range SS-4s, and the 3,500 kilometre-range SS-5s. All of Western Europe was within range of Soviet megaton warheads. The bombers were of two types: the Tu-16 Badger and the Tu-22 Blinder.

While the SS-3 missiles were withdrawn, the increasingly vulnerable SS-4s and SS-5s were kept. By the mid-'60s, the

Soviet Union had already tried to resolve the vulnerability problem by developing two new mobile land-based missiles, the SS-14 MRBM and the SS-15 IRBM. However, they seem to have been technological failures, so neither were deployed. Consequently, intercontinental SS-11 missiles were deployed in the theatre role, later also SS-19s. At the same time, these deployments appeared to compensate for the transfer of a quarter of the SS-4/SS-5 force to the Chinese border in 1968. Today, 120 SS-11s and 60 SS-19s are deployed at SS-4/SS-5 sites in Derazhnya and Pervomaysk.[7] The mobile, intercontinental SS-16 missile, which was prohibited by SALT I, finally gave rise to the famous SS-20, deployed from 1977 on: the SS-20 basically consists of the two first stages of the SS-16.

For intelligence services and military experts, the introduction of the SS-20 was therefore no surprise. On the contrary, it was technologically overdue. Furthermore, it fitted existing military doctrine. Theatre nuclear missiles had already been targeted on military-economic centres (like ports and industrial centres), military and political command and control facilities, and on strategic nuclear force components (like airfields, nuclear weapon depots and detection and warning systems). So while the SS-20 meant a leap upward in counterforce capability, it represented no radical departure in doctrine. Both technologically and doctrinally, the phasing in of SS-20s was a 'natural' move. In all likelihood, the decision seemed easy and to a large extent might have been made automatically without much consideration of its impact on international affairs. However, for many Western political circles, the new missiles became a sign of Soviet threat and aggressiveness. At a time of increasing East-West tension, exaggerations of the threat—both unintentional and deliberate—were only to be expected.

For more than two years after the first SS-20s were deployed, the Soviet Union neither took a major initiative nor made a major political statement on LRTNFs. When Brezhnev finally spoke in Berlin on 6 October 1979, he offered too little too late. Too little, because the offer to reduce the number of launchers did not preclude an increase in the number of warheads targeted on Western Europe. Too late, because in essence, NATO's December 12th decision was already fixed. Had the Soviet Union, for instance, as a follow up to Breżhnev's Bonn visit in June 1978 where LRTNFs figured prominently on the agenda, promised that it would not deploy more warheads on SS-20s than it would eliminate by removing old SS-4 and SS-5 missiles, the whole debacle might have been avoided. Then the so-called zero option (defined as an arrangement which would make deployment of new missiles to Western Europe superfluous) could have already become reality.[8] At that stage, however, Soviet leaders do not seem to have been sufficiently geared to the political aspects and consequences of their SS-20 deployments. The concerns of leaders in East and West were, in other words, badly synchronised: while it was a matter of course for Soviet leaders, the introduction of the SS-20 caused Western leaders to 'rediscover' the Soviet missile threat. In the West, the SS-20 was presented as a grave, new threat—erroneously so—while in the East, there was no political activity to allay the fears, which was also a major blunder.

However, while the historical perspective is necessary to assess current problems, it does not provide comfort. The SS-20s create a feeling of inferiority and insecurity in Western Europe, and they can be used for intimidation and blackmail. In times of war, Soviet doctrine emphasises initiative, surprise, deep strikes and massive use, and such moves can now be executed with greater precision. It is small comfort then that this has been Soviet doctrine for 20 years, that Western Europe has lived under the shadow of Soviet medium- and intermediate-range missiles ever since the end of the '50s and that the threat was 'rediscovered' in 1977 with the deployment of the SS-20s and the deterioration of East-West relations in general.

THE MILITARY-STRATEGIC CASE FOR CRUISE AND PERSHING MISSILES

The official military-strategic justification for deploying cruise and Pershing missiles in Western Europe hinges on the coupling argument and the maintenance of the US *nuclear umbrella* over Western Europe.[9] The following is an attempt to present a rationale for the new missiles along those lines, without pretending that Western defence officials would necessarily subscribe to all of it. It is necessary to undertake this exercise because official statements have tended to lack cogency, clarity and consistency.

If cruise and Pershing missiles are based in Western Europe, a pressure will arise to fire them before they are captured or destroyed, or in retaliation to Soviet attack by similar weapons. Both cruise and Pershing missiles would reach targets on Soviet territory, the maximum range being 2,500 kilometres for the cruise and 1,800 kilometres for the Pershing II. Based in the southwestern part of West Germany (in the Schwäbisch-Gmünd — Neu Ulm — Neckarsulm area), the Pershing missiles would reach almost as far as Moscow.[10] There would, in other words, be an American nuclear attack on the Soviet Union, and the likely response would be a Soviet retaliation against US territory which would mean an escalation of warfare to the strategic level. This is consistent with traditional West German and other NATO strategic theology: for the European countries, nuclear weapons are primarily political weapons, their only rational function being that of dissuasion by deterrence, and a credible threat of rapid escalation to the strategic level would be the most effective deterrent. Cruise and Pershing missiles serve precisely that function, because they will couple the tactical nuclear forces in Europe with the strategic nuclear forces of the United States. Therefore, even though the US nuclear umbrella over Western Europe (the anticipated use of US nuclear forces against the Soviet Union in defence of Western Europe) has been questioned ever since the advent of Soviet intercontinental missiles and more so since the Soviet Union achieved nuclear parity, it would be re-enforced or re-established.

Land-based missiles are, furthermore, more effective in the coupling role than sea-based missiles would be. Submarine-based weapons could be withheld in relatively invulnerable positions for a long period of time, so the pressure to use them at an early stage might be less and the escalatory effect thus more uncertain. Moreover, land-based missiles are more visible than sea-based ones and therefore can be seen by the public to be more *credible* couplers of US and European fortunes. This psychologico-political argument loomed large in the justification for land-basing before the so-called 'dual-track' decision was made on 12 December 1979.[11]

The basing areas in Western Germany maximise the coupling effect. Like the Pershing II, the cruise missiles will move around in *western* parts of West Germany, and the key points are the Hahn, Ramstein and Spangdahlem airfields used by the US, and the Bruggen and Laarbruch airports used by the UK.[12] If the scenario is a European war between the two alliances, it is reasonable to assume that nuclear weapons have already been used when Soviet forces eventually reach the deployment areas of cruise and Pershing missiles, i.e., before they *have* to be fired. The first use of nuclear weapons which is a very hard decision to make, is therefore likely to be a fait accompli. Further use of nuclear arms is usually assumed to be easier to authorise. Since launching cruise and Pershing missiles is not likely to be a question of first use, firing them becomes more thinkable and, consequently, more likely to happen. Seen from the USSR, the threat of retaliation against Soviet territory becomes more credible and the deterrence effect all the more formidable.

The deterrence threat of retaliation against Soviet territory may also be enhanced in another way. It is sometimes argued that it may work like this: if highly accurate nuclear missiles are launched against the USSR from Western Europe, the Soviet Union would retaliate against Western Europe and not against US territory, for fear that its less accurate missiles would lead to an all-out strategic war if launched against the United States. And the more likely it becomes that Soviet retaliation will be directed against Western Europe, the higher the probability is that the US will actually use the new cruise and Pershing missiles against targets on Soviet soil. Thus, Soviet territory would not be a sanctuary in a European war. The Supreme Allied Commander in Europe, General Bernard Rogers, has underlined this deterrent model by emphasising that the Soviet Union would know 'from where we shoot' and by implication, also where to retaliate. But this proposition (which may be thought a particularly

71

American view of LRTNFs) is clearly incompatible with the rationale outlined above (which is a more European view of the matter).

A key factor in this reasoning is *high accuracy*. The Circular Error Probable (CEP) for cruise and Pershing missiles is some tens of metres only (i.e. half of them or more are expected to land that distance from their targets or closer). The Pershing II, with radar terminal guidance (RADAG), has achieved an accuracy as high as 25 metres during tests, so even with a low yield nuclear warhead it will be a most effective counterforce weapon. Yields as low as 1 kiloton have been mentioned, so the collateral damage may be relatively low.[13] The Soviet Union, which is unable to retaliate with similar high accuracy, low yield weapons against US territory, may therefore respond by turning its less accurate weapons against Western Europe. In this case, Western Europe would be hostage and eventually victim of a US nuclear attack on the European part of the USSR—a situation similar to that which existed before the advent of Soviet intercontinental forces, when Soviet LRTNFs were deployed to compensate for the missile gap (which was real enough, but in favour of the US). The other side of this deterrent sword in American premises is therefore the Europeanisation of nuclear war.

This is not the first time the United States has tried to capitalise upon its lead in missile accuracy to bolster European belief in the nuclear umbrella. When former Secretary of Defence Schlesinger presented his nuclear weapons targeting and employment policy in 1974 which was spelled out in National Security Decision Memorandum 242, selective use of strategic weapons against Soviet territory was one of the new features. The selective options were justified by reference to the need to strengthen the umbrella over Europe.[14] Accuracy was a key factor in the strategy of selective options, and since the USSR could only retaliate by means of less accurate missiles with higher yield warheads, it was claimed that the selective options strategy was credible. An attack on Western Europe could, in other words, lead to the use of US strategic weapons in a selective mode. In conclusion, the strategy would therefore create a stronger link between TNFs in Europe and US strategic weapons, thereby enhancing deterrence.

The new feature in relation to the cruise and Pershing missiles is, therefore, not the effort to capitalise on the lead in missile accuracy, but the forward basing of the missiles to Western Germany, Italy, the United Kingdom and other European countries. Land-basing is more visible than sea-basing also because the Soviet Union will be in a better position to determine which types of forces are used with regard to LRTNFs from Western Europe as against strategic forces covered by SALT from the sea. This fits the second deterrence model mentioned above, insofar as it makes it easier to distinguish the beginnings of a theatre nuclear war in Europe from the start of a strategic nuclear exchange between the two superpowers.

These are the main elements of the official NATO and Western European military-strategic rationale for deploying new missiles in Europe. How valid are they?

THE NUCLEAR UMBRELLA OVER WESTERN EUROPE

The role of nuclear weapons in the defence of Western Europe has been problematic ever since the Soviet Union achieved a potent second-strike capability against the USA. In taking France out of NATO's military organisation, de Gaulle argued that no American President would sacrifice Chicago for Paris. The umbrella was gone. At the time, his judgment was disputed. However, with the advent of strategic parity, more and more politicians and observers drew the conclusion that the nuclear umbrella of the '50s had become a fiction.

For the Soviet leadership, the detonation of a US nuclear weapon on Soviet territory is certainly a strategic act. The planned response can hardly depend on the launching point or physical characteristics of the delivery vehicle (such as its accuracy). Retaliation against US territory must be assumed to follow. Is it possible to imagine that the Soviet leaders would, in effect, signal to the Americans that 'our homeland is divisible: if you shoot at us West of the Urals from Western Europe we will leave your territory intact, but not if you use Poseidon or Minuteman missiles'? That does not belong to the rules of the game. Not that retaliation against the US, with the inherent danger of escalating strategic warfare, is necessarily a rational reaction. But the US government can hardly be expected to gamble on the possibility that the Soviet leaders would scrap their planned response and switch to another standard of rationality at the moment of showdown.

In all likelihood, the nuclear umbrella over Western Europe is just as dead as Henry Kissinger said it was in his speech in Brussels in 1979.[15] No technological fix can revive it. Thus, in response to Schlesinger's selective options, the Soviet Union probably prepared measured counterattacks against US territory, for instance, detonation of a similar number of nuclear warheads over deserts or thinly populated areas, to avoid great damage to cities and industrial centres and thereby limit the escalatory effect of the response. Shooting cruise and Pershing missiles from Western Europe makes no basic difference: that would also be a nuclear attack on the Soviet homeland and a dramatic act of irrationality since retaliation against the US is likely to follow.

Therefore, none of the coupling and deterrence assumptions discussed above hold water. On the contrary, to use the new missiles against the Soviet Union and consciously escalate the war to strategic level is something the US would do its utmost to prevent: if there is any supreme national interest, it must be the desire to keep one's own country outside the area of direct nuclear warfare. To launch an attack from Western Europe on the assumption that the Soviet Union would then conveniently retaliate against Western Europe and the US forces there, rather than against US territory, is wishful thinking; it is so obviously so that US decision-makers must have had a clear understanding of it for a long time already. There will never be a mutual agreement between the two superpowers on confining a nuclear war to Europe, between the Atlantic and the Urals, leaving the US as a sanctuary.

A European theatre comprising all European countries except the Soviet Union and the US (which is a European power by invitation) is quite another matter. Should war break out between the military alliances in Europe, both

74

superpowers would, of course, do their very best to keep their own territories out of it. Here, the logic is overwhelming; we don't have to read public statements or war manuals to know that this is so. Precisely because the logic is so compelling, there is no need for superpower talks to establish agreement on it. That community of interests works perfectly well by tacit understanding. This is, take note, not to say that the war will actually be confined, only that the superpowers will *try* to confine it. Nobody can know whether they will succeed: technological mishaps, a chaotic battlefield and human behaviour under extreme stress defy predictability. However, improvements in command, control and communications systems indicate that the technical feasibility of confining a war to Europe is increasing.

Nor is an ambitious US strategic programme likely to revive the nuclear umbrella. Admittedly, the Reagan administration is aiming towards some kind of military superiority in this decade. Depending on the degree and kind of superiority that will eventually be achieved, perceptions of US aims, plans and readiness for action are likely to change, and aggressive US behaviour in various parts of the world might be expected. But much more is needed to revive the umbrella and enable the US to realistically use cruise and Pershing missiles against the Soviet Union in defence of Western Europe. The relationship between the superpowers would have to revert to what it was at the time of the Cuban missile crisis in 1962, and that is out of the question.

It is enough to add that, apart from first use, the decision to launch nuclear weapons against the adversary is likely to be the hardest one to make in a nuclear war. For the Soviet Union to try to capture or destroy cruise and Pershing missiles, or to use its LRTNFs against Western Europe in the massive, deep-strike fashion prescribed by Soviet doctrine, would certainly also be a very dramatic act. However, from a superpower point of view, it would be less consequential than escalation to strategic level. No US superiority is likely to change that in the foreseeable future.

CRUISE AND PERSHING MISSILES IN US STRATEGY

But would there not be pressure on the United States, after all, to fire the missiles before they are captured or destroyed, or in retaliation to a Soviet attack by similar weapons? The answer is yes, the pressure would no doubt be real. So, granted that it is a priority to prevent a nuclear war in Europe from escalating to strategic level, why does the United States invest so much, first of all politically, but also economically, in deploying new missiles to Western Europe? What is the point, in terms of US interests? What is the US military-strategic rationale for wanting the new weapons?

The answer is simple. Should the scenario be that of a European battle, the missiles might well be fired, but most likely against the smaller Eastern European countries, and preferably against Soviet forces, bases and support facilities there. Technologically, there is no problem in using them that way: the minimum range of the Pershing II is 160 kilometres, and cruise missiles can be used over short as well as long distances.[16] Otherwise, if the scenario is not a European battle but a strategic exchange, then cruise and Pershing missiles in Western Europe would be part of the US strategic arsenal, available for use against the Soviet Union in accordance with US strategic warfare plans.

Following this line of reasoning, the *targeting policy* for the cruise and Pershing missiles will comprise alternative sets of targets, tailored to different war scenarios. In a European battle, the missiles are likely to be directed at Eastern Europe; in a strategic exchange, at the Soviet Union. They would figure in US strategic planning as well as in NATO's nuclear warfare plans. A historical precedent for such a solution might be recalled: the Mace B 2,500 kilometre-range cruise missiles deployed to West Germany in the period 1962-1969 were reportedly targeted by the NATO command in Europe against Eastern European countries and by the US Strategic Air Command against the Soviet Union. By fixing alternative sets of targets, a targeting policy for the new missiles may therefore be agreed upon. But a mutually agreed *employment policy* (specifying under which circumstances and for what purposes the missiles should be used) is much less likely to see the light of day. That has always been provisional, procedural or simply unfinished business with NATO's Nuclear Planning Group.[17]

The Pershing II will be one of the most capable counter-force weapons in the American arsenal should it ever come to Europe; the flight time would be 12 minutes or less (depending on distance to target), which means practically no warning time for the Soviet Union. So far, there is no effective defence against ballistic missiles coming down the atmosphere at several times the speed of sound, and the RADAG guidance system makes it effective against virtually any kind of fixed target. Moreover, the range of the Pershing can be extended even further, bringing Soviet ICBM fields in south-western Siberia within reach. Finally, it is claimed that the technological basis exists for installing a terminal guidance system which would make it effective against mobile targets as well, such as SS-20 transport-launcher vehicles in motion.[18] US decision-makers might hope that once introduced, both cruise and Pershing missiles can be replaced by new generations without stirring up much political trouble, in other words, that follow-on versions may prove politically less spectacular.

During 1980, proposals for far more than 572 missiles (ranging up to 1,000 cruise missiles and 300 Pershings) were aired from the other side of the Atlantic. For the time being, these proposals are in abeyance; repeating them would only make it more difficult for European governments to stand by the 1979 decision. However, the Reagan administration may still like to consider the 572 missiles as only the beginning.[19] Political constraints may change, for better or worse, and in the pursuit of military superiority, utilisation of forward bases makes sense. The SS-20 does not reach the US, but forward-based cruise and Pershing missiles can strike against the USSR, so 1,000 missiles on each side in Europe means an 'advantage' of 1,000 for the US in the strategic relationship with the USSR. Should things develop into a 'eurostrategic' arms race, the Soviet Union could, in other words, be left at a significant disadvantage. In the present state of high superpower tension and rivalry, the US may therefore see the 1979 decision as a basis for further developments in LRTNFs while the Soviet leaders may have to face severe boomerang effects from their SS-20 programme.

LRTNFS AND PRESIDENTIAL DIRECTIVE 59

In December 1979 NATO took the LRTNF decision; in summer 1980, Presidential Directive 59 became public knowledge, formalising the USA's 'countervailing' nuclear strategy. The two decisions were prepared in parallel. Little is known about the relationship between them. It has been assumed, however, that the countervailing strategy encouraged the decision to deploy new missiles in Europe.

Presidential Directive 59 put stronger emphasis on destruction of military and political command, control and communications facilities, and raised a large demand for new weapons capable of knocking out hard targets. Cruise and Pershing missiles were technologically close at hand; they are both suitable for hard-target missions, and the Pershing II is ideal for use against time-urgent targets.[20] To speed up cruise and Pershing programmes was therefore a logical response to the new requirement as defined by the counter-vailing strategy. The growing interest in the extended 1,800 kilometre-range Pershing II throughout 1978, leading up to the February 1979 contract with Martin Marietta for full-scale development, was hardly caused by the SS-20 alone. Rather, the SS-20 provided a suitable pretext, and the new countervailing strategy an important rationale.

At an early stage, the US Joint Chiefs of Staff wanted an all Pershing force for Western Europe. However, because of competition between the services (the Tomahawk cruise missile being an Air Force weapon, the Pershing belonging to the Army) politics as usual was applied, resulting in the 464/108 mix.[21] The figure 464 refers to the number of cruise missiles to be deployed on 116 launchers (4 missiles per launcher), while the figure 108 refers to the number of Pershing II launchers. A recent production forecast of 631 for Pershing missiles through 1987 indicates either planned reload capabilities, or deployment of Pershing IIs in countries other than West Germany as well.[22] The 108 Pershing Ia launchers with the US forces in Germany today are prepared for rapid reload and refiring of missiles, and the same launchers will be adopted for use by the Pershing II.[23] Rapid reloading is certainly more realistic for the Pershing II than for the SS-20.

However, in relation to the total demand for new weapons raised by the countervailing strategy, the LRTNF decision of 1979 constitutes a partial, small-scale response only. While taking the new missiles into account, US strategic planners might not want to rely on them for any single mission, since there are alternative, non-strategic uses for the same weapons as well.

DIVERGING INTERESTS ACROSS THE ATLANTIC

For Helmut Schmidt and other Western European leaders voicing their concern over the Soviet LRTNFs and trying, in particular to limit the SS-20 programme, the possibility of new US missile deployments to Western Europe was a political bargaining card. It was a threat that might restrain the new Soviet programmes. In this sense, the quest for new missiles was originally more a Western European than an American demand. However, by the end of 1978, the US appeared to have developed a *military* interest, of their own, in deploying new missiles in Europe. At the NPG meeting in Homestead, Florida, in June 1979, the US weapons-mix proposal was presented to the Europeans almost as a matter of fact. At this stage, the essence of the final decision seems to have been determined. For the last couple of years, the emphasis has therefore differed on the two sides of the Atlantic: the Western Europeans are primarily interested in getting new missiles to Western Europe.

Once more, therefore, it proved difficult to get rid of a 'bargaining chip'. The West German government might, in effect, have tried to become the first one in history to make use of a bargaining chip and then get rid of it, but its hand was overplayed by the Americans. Today, it is caught in a European strategic arms game, led by the superpowers. No doubt, the main losers will be the European countries, unless they succeed in calling it off. From a Western European point of view, it is indeed very hard to find a convincing military-strategic rationale for new cruise and Pershing missiles. Not that the postulated coupling and associated deterrent effects can be discarded entirely: the missiles may after all add uncertainty regarding Western responses to an attack by the Warsaw Pact and induce some additional caution on the Soviet side. More effective coverage of military targets in the smaller Eastern European countries, of Soviet forces, bases and support facilities in particular, also has some deterrent effect. However, in the overall analysis, the coupling effect basically turns out to be a myth. Actually, the new missiles make a difficult situation even worse for the Western Europeans. They burden the host countries with a number of high priority nuclear weapon targets and they will guarantee that Western Europe is drawn into a strategic war between the superpowers. Even today, it is highly likely that Western European countries will be involved in such a war. With cruise and Pershing missiles on their soil, that likelihood becomes a certainty. Equally important, but often neglected in the public debate, the Eastern European countries will also have to pay. In a European battle, they are likely to be the nuclear victims of the cruise and Pershing missiles, while the Western Europeans face destruction from SS-20s.

The official NATO theology that preaches the coupling and deterrence effects of the new missiles therefore sustains a myth. The cruise and Pershing missiles are used in an effort to infuse new life, however artificial, into the nuclear umbrella, glossing over diverging national interests across the Atlantic. To make the US commitment more visible and thereby convincing, deployment in a land-based mode was preferred. Far from reassuring the Europeans, however, the visibility made a strong public opposition even more powerful than it would have been if the missiles had gone to sea or been deployed in another less transparent way. For the first time in 20 years, a strong public opinion in Europe is asking for a reduction and elimination of nuclear weapons from this continent. Public opinion seems stronger on the issue than it ever has been since nuclear weapons came to Europe.

TNF NEGOTIATIONS
In view of the preceding analysis, it may be asked why in what follows the discussion concentrates on proposals to

reduce, rather than to eliminate, TNFs. Why cannot progress be made immediately towards the elimination of nuclear weapons from Europe? Desirable as this may be, it is necessary not only to have long-term goals of real disarmament, but also to relate such goals to what is possible in the existing situation. We have to identify what is the best approach among those which are possible, and find ways to urge the negotiations in that direction. But these are not problems which will be eliminated by TNF negotiations, and we shall certainly have to return to them even if the negotiations produce the best possible result. The following three guide-lines are essential for the negotiations to be successful:

— The aim must be to reach agreement on TNF levels that are low enough to avoid deployment of new cruise and Pershing missiles. Negotiating positions which are un-realistic in relation to this demand can only jeopardise the security of European states, and are likely to generate more public opposition than support.

— The terms of the negotiations should be as simple as possible. If they are as complex as the Mutual (and Balanced) Force Reduction talks which have been going on in Vienna since 1973, they are likely to be drawn out, inconclusive and, in effect, counter-productive.

— To begin with, the negotiations should therefore address the most urgent problems, namely the build-up of missiles, and leave more complex issues like medium-range aircraft aside. There is nothing wrong with partial limitations, provided that they curb or reduce real threats.

At the time of writing, there is no agreement on what to negotiate. The 'dual track' decision of 1979 invited the Soviet Union to negotiate on missiles, while the Soviet Union wants to include US forward-based systems plus British and French forces as well. The counting units also have to be determined.

Here, there seem to be three possibilities: to count launch-ers, missiles or warheads. There are arguments for all of them. Launchers have been on the counting unit in SALT, and are the easiest to verify. Missiles make sense because there are four missiles per cruise launcher, and reload and refire possi-bilities for the ballistic missile launchers. However, missiles are extremely hard to verify, and as a matter of face, none of the parties has shown much interest in making missiles the primary counting unit. In a way, warheads would be the best counting unit, because it is the warheads that kill, not the launchers or the missiles. Warheads have been much emphasised in the West recently, mainly because the SS-20 has been tested in a MIRV mode while cruise and Pershing missiles carry single warheads only. However, if British (and French) forces are included, multiple warheads on SLBMs will make warhead counting disadvantageous for the West.

Altogether, the following systems could be negotiatable:
— Cruise and Pershing missiles planned for Western Europe.
— SS-4 and SS-5 missiles in the Western districts of the USSR, and SS-20 missiles deployed in the same districts and behind the Urals. The missiles behind the Urals are in a 'swing' position between Europe and China, and some of them are likely to be targeted on the Middle East as well. However, they are all capable of hitting Western Europe. The SS-20s in Eastern Siberia may reach the Eastern part of Turkey (and Alaska), but it would be far-fetched to bring them into the European calculus.
— British and French forces. In the early 1990s, Trident SLBMs may give Britain more than 500 independently targetable warheads while the French force, which will improve more rapidly than the British, may be somewhat larger.
— The 180 SS-11s and SS-19s in the European theatre role, Yankee-class submarines which can use their missiles against Europe while in transit to and from stations near the American east coast, and the 400 or so Poseidon warheads assigned to SACEUR for targeting purposes.
— Medium-range aircraft like Soviet Badgers, Blinders and Backfires, possibly also Su-24 Fencer and some MiG-23s, American F-111s, British Vulcans and French Mirage IVs, possibly also American A-6 Intruders, A-7s, Phantoms.
— Forces which can be transferred to Europe on short notice and used in a theatre role, like the US FB-111s and Soviet medium-range aircraft stationed in Siberia.

The negotiations would be much easier and more promising

if they could be confined to the first two or three of these categories. The fact that the French are not willing to take part in the negotiations is not decisive in this connection: their forces can nevertheless be taken into account by allowing Soviet forces to vary with those of the French. Counting rules for that purpose are easy to formulate. To go further down the list would be unnecessary or even counterproductive. The fourth category is already covered by SALT, and the last ones are almost infinitely complex. The combat radius of aircraft depends on flight profile, payload, in-flight refuelling possibilities and availability of airfields, and these are seldom fixed entities.

The prospects for speedy negotiations would therefore be much improved if the aircraft sector is excluded and efforts concentrated on the more urgent missile issues. The fate of the negotiations is linked to the future of SALT anyhow—that much is mutually agreed—so discussion of US forward-based aircraft might be deferred until the SALT talks get moving again. If they are not resumed, it is hardly likely there will be any operative TNF agreement either.

For the Soviet Union, three factors would actually advise against inclusion of bombers: the complexity of the issue, the improvements of air defence systems reducing the penetrability of increasingly old Western aircraft, and the numbers of aircraft involved, which might turn out to be relatively high on the Soviet side. The Soviet Long Range Aviation Force includes, for instance, 450 Badgers and Blinders and about 100 Backfires. Nevertheless, the Soviet Union may prefer a comprehensive approach from the very beginning, because of US efforts to gain some kind of military superiority in this decade. Superiority is not compatible with nuclear arms limitation agreements across the board, only with partial agreements in areas not designated for achieving superiority. As long as that is the perceived context, the Soviet Union is likely to turn a sceptical eye on US proposals for very limited deals.

The US demands for Soviet concessions in Kampuchea and Afghanistan make the prospects even bleaker. In the US view, such concessions are preconditions for agreements on arms limitation. 'Linkage' tends to enhance prevailing trends in international affairs: in the first half of the '70s, linkage politics was a deliberate strategy for promoting East-West cooperation and detente, whereas in recent years it has made tense superpower relations even more intractable. Today, it turns arms limitation into a reward for good behaviour in other fields: if you step down here and there, we offer you mutual arms limitation instead. This is certainly hard to accept for the adversary, and hard to justify before security-minded constituencies in Europe. In reality, arms limitation and disarmament are in the common interest, both of the superpowers and of the other nations of the world. In American politics, however, linkage is deeply rooted, and difficult to get around.

Finally, the introduction of cruise missiles makes it very hard to verify nuclear force deployments. There are different views on the verifiability of agreements concerning land-based cruise missiles, but less so regarding cruise missiles at sea: here, the near unanimous view is that verification becomes impossible. Altogether, the United States is planning to deploy almost 4,000 cruise missiles on board submarines, cruisers, destroyers and battleships during this decade.[24] There will be land-attack versions with conventional as well as nuclear charges, but the external appearance will be the same, so it seems impossible to distinguish between the two. Soviet secretiveness, mutual lack of trust and proliferating cruise missiles therefore raise unprecedented demands for ingenuity in the field of verification techniques. Negotiating treaties sets the highest requirements for verification. This approach to arms limitation and disarmament may therefore be very hard to pursue over the coming years. Unilateral steps and reciprocal action, coordinated through tacit understanding, may yield better results.

UNILATERAL, RECIPROCAL ACTION

Over the last five years, military readiness to produce and deploy new LRTNFs has not been matched by political readiness to seek arms limitations. To a large extent, this period has witnessed a series of mishaps and lost opportunities. We may already have reached a stage at which there are only bad outcomes, and where we must choose the least of all evils.

The negotiations starting at the end of 1981 deserve all our support as long as they have a fair chance of success. However, two years have passed since the 'dual-track' decision was made, and the general prospects for nuclear arms limitations are bleak. The least of the evils may therefore be a unilateral refusal by Western European states to have new cruise and Pershing missiles on their territories. But that may also turn out badly, since it might not have the sobering effect on Soviet military action that Western Europeans, in particular, would like to see. Therefore, it is all the more important to emphasise that unilaterialism can be reciprocal, and that reciprocity can be achieved though tacit understanding. This means there should be East-West consultations to coordinate the moves undertaken by each side. These could make unilateral action more acceptable at home, and therefore easier to decide and implement.

For such an approach to be pursued, some key Western European countries must take the lead. Ostpolitik was pushed by West Germany and France, with a number of more or less sleeping partners elsewhere in Europe. This time, working out a tacit understanding for reciprocal, unilateral action also depends on the right initiatives by a proper combination of countries. Again, West Germany is a country of critical importance.

The key to such a solution might be a Soviet offer not to deploy more warheads on SS-20s than it removes by elimination of old SS-4 and SS-5 missiles, in return for no new cruise and Pershing missiles in Western Europe. The SS-20 force capable of hitting Western Europe is currently at just about that level.

This wouldn't, in itself, improve our situation substantially. However, curbing the incipient growth of eurostrategic missiles is an important prerequisite for real nuclear disarmament, which can make Europe a far more secure place to live.

NOTES

*   This paper is the product of research carried out within SIPRI's project on European Security and Disarmament.

      I am indebted to Per Berg for valuable assistance, especially concerning the history of LRTNFs. The responsibility for the considerations and views expressed in the article rests with the author alone.

1.   In November 1946, six B-29s 'toured' Europe and surveyed airfields for possible use. This is regarded as the first instance in which SAC bombers were used as an instrument of international diplomacy. See US Air Force, SAC, HQ, Office of the Historian: *Development of Strategic Air Command 1946–1976*, Washington D.C.: USAF, 1976; p. 5.

      During the Berlin crisis of 1948, 90 B-29s were forward-based to Europe, but none of these could carry atomic bombs.

2.   Knaack, Marcell Size, *Encyclopaedia of US Air Force Aircraft and Missile Systems, Vol. 1, Post-World War II Fighters, 1945–1973*, Washington D.C., Office of Air Force History, 1978, p. 36.

3.   Haglund, Curt, *Tillbakablick pa utvecklingen av ballistiska robotar i USA samt systembeskrivningar*, Stockholm, FOA 2, 1972, (FOA 2 Rapport A 2552-D9, F5), pp. 3–4.

4.   In addition to the Matador, two intercontinental cruise-missile projects were initiated by the USAF in 1946/1947. The remarkable *Navaho* combined the outstanding performance parameters of 10,000 kilometre-range, a speed of Mach 3.25 and an altitude of 60,000 feet; but by the time it reached maturity, the ICBM was known to be feasible, with superior performance, and the project was cancelled.

5.   At peak deployment there were five Mace A and one Mace B squadron in hardened sites in Europe, with 20-50 missiles per squadron. See *Tactical Nuclear Weapons: European Perspectives*, Taylor & Francis, London, 1978, Stockholm International Peace Research Institute, p. 125.

6.   On the Thor (WS 315A, later SM-75, subsequently PGM-17A) and Jupiter (SM-78, later PGM-19A) programmes, see Armacost, Michael H., *The Politics of Weapons Innovation: The Thor-Jupiter Controversy*, N.Y. and London, Columbia University Press, 1969. See also Polmar, Norman, *Strategic Air Command. People, Aircraft and Missiles*, Cambridge, 1979.

7.   Garthoff indicates that the number of ICBMs designated for the European theatre has been in the range of 180-360. See Garthoff, Raymond L., 'Brezhnev's Opening: The TNF Tangle', *Foreign Policy*, Winter 1980–81.

      The allocation of ICBMs for theatre missions was most probably an interim measure. SS-11s and 19s in this role are therefore likely to be replaced by SS-20s.

8.   The 'zero-option' is differently defined by different prople. Sometimes it is taken to mean no cruise missiles, no Pershing IIs and no SS-20s. At other times it simply means an arrangement which makes cruise missiles and Pershing IIs superfluous. I use the term in the second of these senses.

9.   In public discussions, the need for new LRTNFs has largely been ascribed to the Soviet build-up of SS-20s and Backfire bombers. This line of thought is too superficial. See Peter Cortier, 'Modernization of Theatre Nuclear Forces and Arms Control', *NATO Review*, No. 4, 1981.

10.   The Pershing II will be placed with the 56th field artillery brigade presently operating the Pershing Ia, and be deployed in the same areas.

11.   The 'doppelbeschlus' or 'dual track' decision is so-called because the December 1979 decision by NATO was both to deploy cruise and Pershing

II, and to seek arms control talks with the USSR on LRTNFs.

12. *STERN,* Vol. 34, No. 9, 19 February, 1981.
13. Two warheads are being planned for the Pershing II: an air-burst or surface-burst weapon which will be an adaptation of the already developed B-61 bomb, and an earth-penetrator warhead which '. . . provide a means of attacking hardpoint and subsurface targets with maximum damage and minimum fallout'. Both warheads 'have been selected to capitalize on Pershing II's-accuracy'. Hearings before a subcommittee of the Committee on Appropriations, House of Representatives, February, 1979, p. 863.
14. For an evaluation of the doctrine announcement, see *SIPRI Yearbook 1975,* The MIT Press, Cambridge, Massachusetts, and London, England, Stockholm International Peace Research Institute, pp. 41–46.
15. Opening address at the conference on 'NATO, The Next Thirty Years', Brussels, September 1-3, 1979.
16. *World Missile Forecast,* June, 1981.
17. Uwe Nerlich, 'Theatre Nuclear Forces in Europe: Is NATO Running Out of Options?', *The Washington Quarterly,* Vol. 3, No. 1, Winter, 1980.
18. Robert A. Moore, 'Theatre Nuclear Forces. Thinking the unthinkable', *International Defense Review,* Vol. 14, No. 4, 1981.
    A further-developed version of the Pershing with a range of about 4,000 kilometres is in 'technology development', so far under limited funding.
19. For US rearmament proposals put forward in this period, see *Independence Through Military Strength. A Program for Forces to Preserve and Extend American Freedom 1980-85,* The Institure of American Relations, Washington, February 22, 1980, and *National Security in the 1980s: From Weakness to Strength,* Institute for Contemporary Studies, San Francisco, California, 1980.
20. 'Potential Pershing II targets include: hardened and soft missile sites; airfields; naval bases; nuclear, biological and chemical storage sites; command and control centers; headquarters; rail yards; road networks/choke points; ammunition and petroleum storage facilities; troop concentrations and facilities; and dams/locks. Pershing II is particularly effective against hard point and underground targets because of its high accuracy and the unique earth penetrator warhead capability'. Secretary Alexander before the Subcommittee of the Committee on Appropriations, *op. cit.*
21. See Fred Kaplan in *New York Times Magazine,* December 10, 1979.
22. *World Missile Forecast,* June, 1981.
23. In 1976, units in Europe received the first of a further advanced Automatic Azimuth Reference System/Sequential Launch Adapter, which enables one commander to fire up to three Pershing Ia missiles in succession and to shoot after only brief delay from a previously unsurveyed site.
    While Pershing Ia crews must count down and launch the missiles in sequence, Pershing II gear will allow the simultaneous check-out and launch of three rounds. See Doug Richardson, 'Pershing II–NATO's smart ballistic missile', *Flight International,* 8 August, 1981.
24. See, e.g. Michael Getler, 'Cruise Missiles Eyed for Ships and Subs; Arms Curbers Uneasy', *Washington Post,* 7 August, 1981.

THEATRE NUCLEAR WEAPONS:
THE SOVIET DOCTRINE

David Holloway

In the controversy aroused by the NATO decision of December 1979 much has been written about Western conceptions of the role of theatre nuclear forces (TNF) in deterrence and in war. But, although the NATO decision has been justified in terms of the Soviet deployment of the Tu-22M Backfire bomber and the SS-20 intermediate-range ballistic missile (IRBM), little attention has been paid to Soviet thinking about TNF. This is surprising, because the reason why the NATO decision has caused concern is not merely that new missiles will be deployed, but rather that this decision is linked with shifts in Western strategic thinking, and in particular with an apparent readiness on the part of the United States to contemplate fighting a 'limited' nuclear war in Europe. When NATO decided to deploy the new weapons in Europe, it also undertook to try to negotiate limitations on TNF, and West European governments have laid special emphasis on this aspect of policy. But it takes two to wage limited nuclear war, and it takes two to negotiate arms limitations. Soviet thinking on these topics needs therefore to be examined. This article tries to provide a general introduction to Soviet views, but does not claim to offer a comprehensive analysis of a difficult area.

TNF AS A CATEGORY
The first problem is that of definition. It is only in recent years that theatre nuclear weapons have come to be treated as a separate category. Previously the acronym TNW was used to refer to 'tactical nuclear weapons'. But this term had its critics, especially in the Soviet Union. A leading Soviet commentator on military affairs, M. Milshtein, wrote in the late 1970s that

the term 'tactical nuclear weapons' is a very conditional and vague term; it does not really reflect either the potential of these weapons or their specifications. Moreover it has only a one-sided meaning—they are tactical only with respect to the USA. As for the countries on whose territory these weapons may be used, they are essentially strategic weapons because their use would lead to disastrous consequences.[1]

This last point has been made repeatedly by the Soviet Union, which has claimed that American 'tactical nuclear weapons' deployed in Europe should be counted as strategic systems if they can strike Soviet territory. This problem of definition has considerable practical significance, for systems of this kind, known as forward-based systems (FBS), proved to be a contentious issue at SALT I and SALT II. The Soviet Union argued that they should be counted against the ceilings for US Strategic forces, while claiming that its own medium-range and intermediate-range ballistic missiles (MR/IRBMs) and medium-range bombers should not be counted as strategic systems for the purposes of SALT because they could not reach American territory.[2]

Milshtein goes on to argue that in relation to the Central European theatre the most suitable term for TNWs is 'theatre nuclear weapons'. This would cover 'the nuclear weapons that are deployed, could be deployed, or are intended for use in the theatre of hostilities', irrespective of the yield and range of the weapons.[3] This definition has its uses, but points to further problems. If all nuclear weapons intended for use in a theatre are defined as theatre nuclear weapons, does it make sense to seek a balance in Long-Range Theatre Nuclear Forces (LRTNF), without reference to shorter-range systems, given that both may be intended for use in the same theatre, and that their missions and targets may overlap (for example, interdiction or destruction of large troop concentrations)?

Milshtein notes that the definition of TNW as 'theatre nuclear weapons' leaves certain grey areas, and mentions the US missile-carrying submarines assigned to NATO and the British bombers intended for use in the Central European theatre in this category; the Soviet Backfire bomber and the SS-20 might also be added. Milshtein is certainly not implying that a nuclear war in Europe can be confined to a specific theatre. Indeed, if systems based outside the theatre are intended for use inside the theatre, would this not lead to an almost automatic escalation of the conflict? The question of escalation is central to the current controversy because many Europeans fear that a limited nuclear war is conceived of as possible by military planners in the United States and the Soviet Union. The Soviet attitude toward limited nuclear war will be looked at later. The point to note here is that the category of LRTNF is not clear-cut and cannot properly be considered in isolation from other nuclear forces.

THE DEVELOPMENT OF SOVIET THEATRE NUCLEAR FORCES

The Red Army's victorious advance to Berlin in 1945 liberated Eastern Europe from Nazi rule and ensured Soviet dominance in the area. The presence of the Red Army in Eastern Europe enhanced Soviet security against the kind of attack that Hitler had launched with such devastating effect on 22 June 1941. But this gain was partly offset by the American atomic bomb, which posed a new threat to Soviet security. By 1946 Stalin had initiated major programmes to develop nuclear weapons, long-range rockets, radar and jet propulsion. These were designed to provide the Soviet Union with its own nuclear weapons and means of delivery, and also with defence against American air power. But the chief instrument of Soviet military power was the Army, which remained in Eastern Europe in significant numbers, and was regarded as providing the main counterweight to the American atomic monopoly. Although the Soviet Union tested an atomic bomb in 1949, it was not until 1953 that the Armed Forces acquired nuclear weapons.

In the mid-1950s the Soviet Armed Forces began to acquire a stockpile of nuclear weapons and the means to deliver them. These delivery systems were of various ranges: medium (or regional, or theatre), intercontinental and short. In 1954 the Tu-16 Badger medium-range bomber entered service, and in the following year the SS-3 MRBM began to be deployed. In 1956 two intercontinental bombers, the Mya-4 Bison and the Tu-95 Bear, entered service. From 1957 the Ground Forces began to acquire short-range tactical and operational-tactical missiles (FROG and SCUD) for use on the battlefield.

In August 1957 the Soviet Union conducted the first successful flight test of an ICBM, the SS-6. In October this rocket was used to launch Sputnik 1. In spite of this dramatic demonstration that the United States was now vulnerable to attack by Soviet nuclear weapons, it was not until the 1960s that the Soviet Union began to acquire a major intercontinental force. In the late 1950s Soviet policy concentrated on the deployment of systems that could deliver nuclear weapons against targets in and around Europe (and in other regions on the Soviet periphery). Deployment of the SS-4 MRBM began in 1959, and of the SS-5 IRBM in 1961. In the early 1960s the Tu-22 Blinder medium-range bomber entered service. In 1965 the Soviet Union had 773 MR/IRBMs (SS-3, SS-4 and SS-5) and 880 medium-range bombers (Tu-16 and Tu-22), as compared with 224 ICBMs and 195 intercontinental bombers.

This early stress on the deployment of theatre systems was not anticipated by the United States in the 1950s, and the expectation that the Soviet Union would give priority to intercontinental systems contributed to the 'bomber-gap' and 'missile-gap' scares of the period. The early emphasis on medium-range forces is sometimes forgotten now, but it was the logical pattern of development for the Soviet Union to pursue. It was easier from a technical point of view to develop medium-range rather than intercontinental systems. (Indeed, two of the early intercontinental systems—the Mya-4 Bison bomber and the SS-6 ICBM—seem to have suffered from technical drawbacks.) A more important consideration, however, was the fact that many of the nuclear weapons that could threaten the Soviet Union were based in or around Europe, while others might be redeployed to the area in the event of war. This consideration was particularly important because Soviet military thinking regarded nuclear weapons much as it did other weapons. In the event of war the mission of the Soviet Armed Forces would be to destroy the enemy's forces and war-fighting capacity, and not merely to inflict unacceptable damage to his society. It made sense, therefore, to give greater priority to systems that could destroy NATO forces, which directly threatened the Soviet Union, than to systems that could destroy American cities.[4]

In a survey of post-war Soviet military art Major-General Cherednichenko notes that in the mid-1950s it was assumed that a new world war would inevitably be a nuclear war—a reasonable assumption in view of the contemporary American doctrine of massive retaliation. In such a war nuclear strikes against military-economic centres, communications, command and administrative centres and enemy strategic nuclear forces would acquire great significance.[5] It is plausible to assume that these were the targets for Soviet medium-range systems at the time. Short-range missiles were intended for use on the battlefield against enemy tactical nuclear weapons and troop formations. It is true that in his nuclear diplomacy Khrushchev threatened France and Britain with destruction by nuclear weapons. Nevertheless, Cherednichenko's list of targets is interesting because it indicates the direction of Soviet military thinking, and Soviet military writing suggests that the general categories in the present Soviet target list are likely to be the same.[6]

From the mid-1960s Soviet policy concentrated on the deployment of an intercontinental force. It was not until the mid-1970s that new purpose-built theatre nuclear forces were deployed. Yet in the 1960s Soviet medium-range forces faced two major problems. The first was the transformation of the Sino-Soviet conflict into a military confrontation. This placed greater demands on Soviet theatre forces, and was tackled by redeploying some systems to the East in 1968. The second problem was the increasing vulnerability of the SS-4s and SS-5s to attack by American nuclear forces. In the age of reconnaissance satellites the launch sites for these weapons could be located, and the missiles were not protected by super-hardened silos. The Soviet Union tried to resolve this problem in the mid-1960s by developing two new mobile land-based missiles, the SS-14 MRBM and the SS-15 IRBM. But these developments were not successful, apparently for technical reasons, and were not deployed in any numbers. The variable-range SS-11 ICBM was adapted for a theatre role; by the early 1970s some 120 of these systems had been deployed in SS-4 and SS-5 missile fields in the western Soviet Union.[7]

In the mid-1970s the Soviet Union began to deploy the Tu-22M Backfire bomber and the SS-20 IRBM. It is these systems that have caught the attention of the West and caused concern about a Soviet TNF build-up. In October 1979 Mr. Brezhnev tried to head off the NATO TNF decision by declaring that the Soviet Union was 'prepared to reduce the number of medium-range nuclear delivery means deployed in the western areas of the Soviet Union as compared with the present level, but of course only in the event that no additional medium-range nuclear delivery means are deployed in Western Europe'.[8] He went on to state 'categorically' that

> the number of medium-range nuclear delivery means on the territory of the European portion of the Soviet Union has not been increased by even one missile, or even one airplane, over the past ten years. On the contrary, the number of launchers of medium-range missiles, and also the yield of the nuclear charges of these missiles, have even been somewhat reduced. The number of medium-range bombers has also been reduced.[9]

Western estimates bear out this contention.[10]

Of course, these figures tell only part of the story, and the number of deliverable warheads (which Mr. Brezhnev did not mention) has not declined over the same period, and is likely to increase as the SS-20 replaces the older missiles. Moreover, the increased range and penetration of the Backfire bomber make it a more effective system than previous medium-range bombers and create new problems for NATO air defences. The mobile SS-20, one model of which carries three warheads, is a much less vulnerable system than the SS-4 and SS-5, and also much more effective because of its increased range and accuracy. The latest generation SS-19 ICBM has been deployed in old SS-11 silos in TNF missile fields, and thus may have a theatre role too; some SLBMs also have a theatre role.

Certainly the new systems increase the Soviet ability to strike targets in Western Europe. These systems also increase the options open to Soviet commanders. Not only would the

SS-20s be more effective than the SS-4 and SS-5 in a surprise attack, but they could also be withheld in the event of a conflict, whereas the vulnerability of the SS-4 and SS-5 would create pressure to use them early on, since withholding them might invite a pre-emptive strike.

SOVIET DOCTRINE

At the end of 1959 the Strategic Missile Forces were established as a separate service, with command of all land-based strategic missiles; by Soviet definition, missiles with a range of 1,000 kilometres or more are strategic. In January 1960 Khrushchev announced a new military doctrine, declaring that a new world war would inevitably be a rocket-nuclear war, which would begin with nuclear strikes deep into the enemy's interior. Preparation for such a war became the central concern of Soviet military policy in the 1960s, not because the Soviet leaders wanted a nuclear war, but because they believed that the best way to prevent war was to prepare to fight it. There was considerable argument about the forces required for a general nuclear war, but no disagreement that such a war should be the main focus of policy and strategy. In the early 1960s little attention was given to preparation for local or limited wars, beyond a general commitment to aid national liberation struggles.[11]

Since that time, however, Soviet thinking has changed, especially in its view of the kinds of war which might occur, and of the ways in which a general war might start. In the late 1960s the Soviet Ground Forces began to train for non-nuclear as well as nuclear operations in Europe. In the 1970s Soviet policy gave increasing attention to the capacity to project military power around the globe.[12] The overall effect of these changes has been to move the focus of policy away from exclusive preoccuaption with general nuclear war. There is now a greater readiness to envisage conflicts of different kinds.

Several factors have contributed to this change. First, the Soviet Union has responded to shifts in world politics, and in particular to the possibility of war with China. The greater complexity of the international system has meant that military thinking has had to turn its attention to wars of various kinds, and not merely to a general nuclear war with the United States. Second, the Soviet Union has responded to NATO's shift towards a strategy of flexible response, which does not envisage that war in Europe will automatically begin as a nuclear conflict. The Soviet Union did not wish to be tied into an inflexible one-variant strategy of its own, and accordingly adjusted its policy to prepare for conventional operations in Europe.

The third factor to influence Soviet views of possible conflicts was the attainment of strategic parity with the United States in the late 1960s. It was on the basis of mutually recognised parity that the Strategic Arms Limitation Talks began in 1969. One consequence of parity has been, in Soviet eyes, to open up greater possibilities for using military force as an instrument of policy outside the central military relationship with NATO. Parity would prevent the West from trying to deal with the Soviet Union from a position of strength, and thus force it to adopt a more accommodating attitude toward Soviet interests. At the same time it would provide an opportunity for the Soviet Union to counter Western power in the Third World, and thus to advance Soviet influence.[13]

A fourth factor appears also to have influenced Soviet views of possible wars. In the 1970s the Soviet leaders came to accept that mutual deterrence, in the sense of mutual vulnerability to devastating nuclear strikes, was the only possible relationship with the United States at present. Strategic parity has become the stated objective of Soviet policy.[14] (It may appear paradoxical that as Soviet military power has grown, so less emphasis has been put on attaining victory in nuclear war. The explanation lies in a growing confidence in the ability of Soviet military power to deter an American attack, coupled with a belief that any attempt to break out of this strategic relationship would be extremely costly and almost certainly ineffective.) Nevertheless, Soviet doctrine has emphasised the need to prepare to fight and win a nuclear war, and Western governments have been alarmed because they see the new Soviet theatre weapons as part of a more general drive for significant military superiority.

It is important to understand that what is going on is not only a competition in armaments, but also in strategies, with each side seeking to make the strategy of the other unworkable. The NATO strategy of flexible response, with its readiness to move from conventional to tactical nuclear and then to strategic nuclear levels of conflict, was devised at a time when NATO had superior tactical and strategic nuclear forces. One of the consequences—and, one may assume, one of the objectives—of the growth of Soviet military power has been to render that doctrine more dubious and problematical than it was when it was first formulated. The entry on 'limited war' in the Soviet Military Encyclopaedia argues that

the Soviet Union's success in creating atomic and thermonuclear weapons and rockets of different kinds, its ability to inflict a retaliatory devastating nuclear strike on the territory of the enemy have made general nuclear war unpromising and very dangerous for the imperialists. This has led to the elaboration of theories of limited war, the implementation of which, in their authors' opinion, ought without special risk to ensure for the USA the attainment of its aggressive goals by means of military operations on others' territory and basically by others' hands.[15]

In the 1970s Soviet commentators have portrayed American theories of limited nuclear war, and American strategies of limited nuclear exchanges, as part of an effort to wriggle out of the consequences of strategic parity and to restore political and military utility to American strategic power.[16]

It is in this context that the Soviet attitude toward TNF can best be understood. First, the latest Soviet systems possess the kind of flexibility which Soviet doctrine now seems to call for. A discrepancy had emerged between the operational characteristics of the SS-4 and SS-5 and Soviet ideas about the course a war in Europe might take. This discrepancy is being eliminated as the newer weapons replace the older ones.

Second, the Soviet attitude toward the new NATO systems is determined not only by the characteristics and numbers of these weapons, but also by the shifts in American thinking to which they appear to be linked. From the Soviet point of view, these systems are not so much an addition to theatre forces as an augmentation of American strategic power. The Pershing II missile is of special significance in this regard, because it is highly accurate and (as a ballistic rather than a cruise missile) could reach Moscow and other targets within range in only four to six minutes. 108 of these missiles, which NATO now plans to deploy, would not by themselves constitute an effective first-strike force. But in the context of American strategic weapons programmes—and in particular of the highly accurate M-X ICBM—Pershing II looks more dangerous. (If, as some Western analysts have suggested, the Soviet Union has a launch-on-warning strategy, Pershing II's short flight time poses a particular threat.[17]) The NATO decision is seen as part of a drive by the United States to achieve strategic superiority over the Soviet Union.

Third, Soviet leaders have said that if the new US systems are deployed in Europe, they will take steps to maintain what they claim is strategic equality. It is not clear how this might be done, but the Soviet Union might try to threaten American territory from bases off the coast (a new Cuban missile crisis?), or deploy additional systems in Europe, perhaps even in Eastern Europe.[18]

This paper has argued that Soviet military policy has been giving more attention than in the early 1960s to the possibility of military actions below the level of general nuclear war, and that Soviet policy has tried to make NATO's strategy of flexible response more problematical. Does this mean that the Soviet leaders think that the American nuclear guarantee to Western Europe is no longer operative? It is difficult to give a categorical answer, but I think not. Soviet military writings still emphasise that the danger of escalation exists:

> Every limited war in contemporary conditions, when the majority of countries are linked among themselves by political and economic agreements, conceals within itself the real danger of growing into world war.[19]

Soviet doctrine is couched in very general terms, so that it says little about the precise conditions under which escalation from conventional to nuclear war might occur. There seems to be little or nothing in Soviet writings to indicate

98

that Soviet leaders think that a nuclear war in Europe could remain limited to the European theatre. The Soviet view of American forward based systems as part of the American strategic arsenal as a whole suggests that no substantial difference would be seen between an attack on the Soviet Union by American nuclear weapons based in Europe and one by nuclear weapons based in the United States or on submarines.

Mr. Brezhnev told the 26th Party Congress in February 1981 that

> A 'limited' nuclear war, as conceived by the Americans in, say, Europe, would from the outset mean certain destruction of European civilisation. And, of course, the United States, too, would not be able to escape the flames of war. (*Pravda*, 24 February 1981)

It is impossible to be definite, however, and it is conceivable that a nuclear exchange might be limited to Europe if Soviet territory were not struck by American nuclear weapons. But in general Soviet thinking has seemed to be more sceptical than American about the possibility of controlling the level of conflict, and if it is believed that a conflict will escalate into general nuclear war, then this might provide the incentive to move first to the use of strategic weapons.

ARMS CONTROL

One of the reasons why the new Soviet systems produced such a shock in Western Europe is that the Soviet missiles deployed in the late 1950s and early 1960s had been widely regarded as a 'quick fix', something to be deployed before intercontinental weapons were ready; they were therefore thought unlikely to be replaced by newer systems. This was, however, a serious misreading of Soviet attitudes. The issue of forward-based systems was a major and contentious one at SALT, until the Vladivostock Accord of 1974 deferred it to a future round of negotiations (and even then it re-emerged as an issue in the talks). The SALT II Treaty Protocol did impose restrictions on the testing and deployment of some types of cruise missile, but this was due to lapse on 31 December 1981 and thus imposed little real restraint on American or Soviet programmes. A letter of agreement also set limits to the rate of production of the Backfire bomber.

When, in spite of the Brezhnev proposal, NATO went ahead with its decision in December 1979, the Soviet Union appeared unwilling to enter negotiations on TNF. But during Chancellor Schmidt's visit to Moscow in July 1980 the Soviet leaders proposed simultaneous negotiations on medium-range missiles and American forward-based weapons, in which the two elements would be 'organically connected'. Such negotiations, the Soviet leaders indicated, could begin without waiting for the ratification of SALT II, but any agreement reached could be put into effect only after SALT II came into force. In October 1980 the United States and the Soviet Union began preparatory talks in Geneva.

These talks, which coincided with the US Presidential election, proved inconclusive, but they did point to the problem of defining what the scope of the negotiations should be. The United States, acting for NATO, insisted that any agreement should cover medium-range missiles, involve '*de jure* equality in both ceilings and rights', and be adequately verifiable. The Soviet Union argued that talks about missiles had to be 'organically linked' with discussions about American FBS. The Soviet Union did not concede that Soviet medium-range aircraft should be included (although it apparently hinted that the Backfire bomber might be put on the agenda), nor that those SS-20s based in the central part of the USSR, and thus capable of striking targets in either Europe or China, should be counted. But the Soviet Union has decided not to raise, at the present stage, the question of British and French nuclear forces.[20]

Since those talks Soviet conditions for an agreement have been modified. At the 26th Party Congress in February 1981 Mr. Brezhnev indicated that the Soviet Union would be willing to renegotiate SALT II, and offered a moratorium on TNF deployment, which NATO has rejected on the grounds that it would merely ratify Soviet superiority and that it would not limit systems capable of striking Europe from east of the Urals.[21] For the purposes of arms control this is an extremely complex issue. There is no agreement on what systems to weigh in the balance. The Soviet Union claims that strategic equality exists in the European theatre, while NATO claims that the Soviet Union enjoys a significant superiority.

Since October 1979 the Soviet Union has conducted an intensive campaign to capitalise on the opposition which the NATO decision has aroused in Western Europe. This campaign undoubtedly has a dual purpose: to prevent the implementation of the NATO plan, and to exacerbate relations between the United States and its West European allies. Paradoxically, the NATO decision, which was seen by the NATO governments as a way of cementing the political cohesion of the alliance after the disarray caused by the neutron bomb issue, has itself become a source of friction within the alliance. Under pressure from the West European governments, the Reagan Administration has agreed to engage in TNF talks with the Soviet Union. The chief motive is the fear that without negotiations the American weapons will not be politically acceptable in Western Europe. This motivation is rather transparent, however, and thus the negotiations may fail to achieve the desired political effort. Moreover, the past record of arms control talks suggests that an agreement is unlikely before the new systems are deployed.

CONCLUSION

This article has tried to provide some pointers towards understanding Soviet thinking on TNF. It has not been able to offer a detailed analysis of the changing military balance, or a critical assessment of Soviet views. Nor has it asked whether the NATO decision has been an appropriate response to Soviet efforts to make NATO strategy unworkable. But it is important to try to understand what Soviet thinking is, for that offers an insight into the way in which Soviet policy develops. For example, the Soviet approach to TNF negotiations clearly follows from the way in which the Soviet Union has viewed American FBS.

The conclusions can be summarised as follows. First, it is essential to grasp how Soviet military thought has categorised these weapons. The Soviet Union has classified the new missiles which NATO proposes to deploy with American FBS which have been stationed in Europe since the late 1940s. The Soviet Union has traditionally seen these as strategic systems because they could strike Soviet territory. This has been a consistent Soviet position, not one fabricated for the purposes of negotiation.

Second, Soviet policy has placed great emphasis on theatre nuclear forces and on the nuclear balance in the European theatre. By the 1970s the systems which had been deployed in the late 1950s and early 1960s were becoming obsolete. Moreover, these systems were not flexible enough for new Soviet thinking about the course of a possible war in Europe. The Soviet Union has claimed that the deployment of its new systems amounts to no more than modernisation of existing forces, and points to the fact that the total number of launchers has not increased as evidence of this.

Third, TNF cannot properly be viewed in isolation from other elements in the military balance. NATO sees the new Soviet theatre weapons as a threatening element in a general build-up of military power, while the Soviet Union regards the NATO decision on TNF as part of a broader shift in policy which poses new threats to the Soviet Union.

Fourth, it should be realised that what is taking place is a competition not only in arms, but also in strategies, with each side seeking to make the strategy of the other un-workable. Soviet policy appears to have been designed to make the NATO strategy of flexible response more problematical than it inherently is. The NATO decision is directed towards ensuring that flexible response, with its threat of escalation up to the strategic level, remains a credible strategy, and that the Soviet Union does not come to believe that the American guarantee to Western Europe has become invalid.

Fifth, partly because Soviet and Western perceptions of the military balance differ so much, the TNF issue is a particularly complex one from the point of view of arms control. SALT took place on the basis of a mutually recognised parity, and yet agreement was hard to achieve. (At the talks on Mutual and Balanced Force Reductions (MBFR) in Europe, which have been going on since 1973, no agreement has yet been reached on the nature of the balance, and hence no treaty has been concluded.) Negotiations about TNF are likely to take place in the context of disagreement about the nature of the balance, and this will make agreement even more difficult. Given the past record of arms control negotiations, it is unlikely that a substantial agreement will emerge quickly from the talks. But the TNF issue may well remain the focus of disagreement and conflict between East and West and within the Western alliance.

NOTES

1. M. Milshtein, 'Tactical Nuclear Weapons: Problems of Definition and Application', in SIPRI, *Tactical Nuclear Weapons: European Perspectives*, Taylor & Francis, London, 1978, p. 173.
2. Thomas W. Wolfe, *The SALT Experience*, (Cambridge, Mass.: Ballinger Publishing Co., 1979), pp. 103–106.
3. M. Milshtein, op. cit., p. 173.
4. On Soviet military thought in the mid-1950s, see Raymond L. Garthoff, *Soviet Strategy in the Nuclear Age* (London: Atlantic Books, Stevens and Sons, Ltd., 1958), especially pp. 61–96.
5. Major-General M. Cherednichenko, 'Ob osobennostyakh razvitiya voennogo iskusstva v poslevoennyi period', *Voenno-istoricheskii zhurnal*, 1970, no. 6, p. 25.
6. See, for example, the statements on the targets for strategic missiles, which, by Soviet definition, include the medium-range missiles targeted on Europe, in V.D. Sokolovskii, *Voennaya strategiya* (Moscow: Voenizdat, 1968), p. 235; *Artilleriya i rakety* (Moscow: Voenizdat, 1968), p. 224.
7. See the discussion in Robert P. Berman and John C. Baker, *Soviet Strategic Forces* (Washington, D.C.: Brookings Institution), forthcoming.
8. *Pravda*, 7 October 1979.
9. Ibid.
10. See Raymond L. Garthoff, 'The TNF Tangle', *Foreign Policy*, No. 41, Winter 1980-81, p. 86.
11. The clearest statement of Soviet strategy at that time is provided by the first edition of Marshal Sokolovskii's *Voennaya strategiya*, published in 1962.
12. For a discussion of these modifications to doctrine see Harriet Fast Scott and William F. Scott, *The Armed Forces of the USSR* (Boulder, Colorado: Westview Press, 1979), pp. 54–59.
13. For further discussion, see David Holloway, 'Military Power and Political Purpose in Soviet Policy', *Daedalus*, Fall 1980, pp. 21–23.
14. Raymond L. Garthoff, 'Mutual Deterrence and Strategic Arms Limitation in Soviet Policy', *International Security*, Summer 1979.
15. *Sovetskaya Voennaya Entsiklopedia*, vol. 6. (Moscow: Voenizdat, 1978), p. 17.
16. See, for example, the commentary by M.A. Milshtein and L.S. Semeiko on the Schlesinger doctrine in *S.Sh.A.*, 1974, no. 11, pp. 2–13.
17. Raymond L. Garthoff, 'The TNF Tangle', pp. 92–93.

18. *The Times,* 26 June 1981.
19. *Sovetskaya Voennaya Entsiklopedia,* vol. 6, p. 18.
20. *Strategic Survey 1980-81* (London: International Institute for Strategic Studies, 1981), pp. 109–110; see also V. Boikov, 'NATO's "forgotten" arsenal of U.S. forward-based weapons', *Soviet News,* 23 September 1980.
21. *Pravda,* 24 February 1981; NATO communique of 5 May 1981, *The Times,* 6 May 1981.

THE ROLE OF NUCLEAR WEAPONS IN WESTERN RELATIONS

Mary Kaldor

In accepting the US security guarantee, the European members of NATO have, in effect, placed incredible trust and confidence in the President of the United States. They have granted him the right to decide whether or not to engage in nuclear war in Europe. Put bluntly, they have abdicated control over European lives. Seen from this perspective, the presence of US troops in Europe is not so much a hostage against the failure of the US Government to act in the event of a Soviet invasion as a hostage against the danger that it might act and initiate a nuclear war.

From the point of view of the ordinary European citizen, however, is it any different for nations who possess independent nuclear forces? Decisions about nuclear weapons are, after all, taken in secret by a very few people. We now know how Attlee railroaded the decision to develop the A-bomb through a small subcommittee of the British cabinet in 1947 and how Callaghan, Healey and Owen secretly went ahead with the Chevaline programme to improve the Polaris warhead during the 1974-79 Labour Government. And in France, according to Alfred Grosser, even

> more than in the United States during the war and Great Britain after it, the activity of a small group of military men and high officials was carried on almost wholly outside the constitutional decision-making process and with an almost total absence of any democratic control.[1]

How much difference does it really make if the power of annihilation is in the hands of the British Prime Minister or the President of France, rather than the President of the United States?

In one very real sense, the ownership and control of nuclear weapons incarnates relationships of power. The moment when Giscard d'Estaing handed to François Mitterrand the codes for launching France's nuclear weapons was considered, by the press and television, to be the moment when Mitterrand became President. Over the years, an elaborate ritual, expressed in the language of deterrence, has been created to justify, explain and cement the pattern of power established by nuclear weapons. And yet, for historical reasons, this pattern does not necessarily correspond to patterns of economic and political power. Indeed, over the years, the ritual has become more and more remote from broader economic and political realities—in particular, the economic rise of Western Europe and Japan, the growing political importance of West Germany, the independence of the Third World, and the widespread popular demand in Western industrialised countries for greater political participation. The danger is that this disjunction could cause war. As the pattern of power delineated by nuclear weapons begins to falter, the ritual could be called to account. The power of nuclear weapons is likely to be increasingly asserted, in the absence of other kinds of economic and political power.

This paper is an attempt to outline the changing relationships between Europe and America and to explain the current debate about nuclear weapons in this context. The causes of the growth of nuclear arsenals are to be found, I believe, in the institutions which create them—in the relationship between arms manufacturers, armed forces, civil servants and scientists. But the doctrine that is developed to justify each new generation of weapons has to be explained in wider political terms. Indeed, in the case of the cruise missile designed for Europe, it is very difficult to see how the doctrine bears any relation to its technical characteristics. This article is about the debate about doctrines. In particular, I want to explore the current divisions in the Socialist and Social Democrat Parties of north western Europe which seem, somehow, to be symbolised in the nuclear issue. The present international crisis is, I believe, fundamentally about the challenge to present patterns of power as they are defined by the ownership and control of nuclear weapons. It is a challenge both from those who wish merely to alter the pattern, to establish a new and perhaps more 'appropriate' ritual, and from those in the growing disarmament movement who reject the ritual altogether, who assert, as fundamental, the individual human right to survive.

In developing this argument, I do not reject the idea of the Soviet threat, but I regard it as *entirely* secondary, now and ever since 1945, to the danger of nuclear war. It is, of course, necessary to defend societies against external military threats and to resist outside interference in political affairs. But this is a matter which is entirely separate from the question of nuclear weapons. The confusion of these two issues, the Soviet threat and the danger of nuclear war, has, as I shall show, been an important and deceptive mechanism for upholding the nuclear ritual.

THE US-EUROPEAN RELATIONSHIP[2]

When NATO was formed in 1949, there were few leaders of opinion who seem to have seriously believed in the possibility of direct Soviet military aggression against Western Europe. This notion only took on substance after the outbreak of the Korean War in the summer of 1950. In March 1949, a month before the creation of NATO, John Foster Dulles said:

> I do not know any responsible official, military and civilian, in this Government or any Government who believes that the Soviet Government now plans conquest by open military means.[3]

And his statement was corroborated by the Secretary of Defense, James V. Forrestal, by the US Ambassador to the Soviet Union, by George Kennan, who was then Director of the Policy Planning Staff at the State Department, as well as others. In my view, the main purposes of NATO lay elsewhere.

The main problem faced by American policy makers after 1945 was how to establish peace and prosperity within the framework of a free enterprise system. The New Dealers, and those that came after them, were deeply convinced that the Depression and the Second World War had been caused by economic nationalism. Commitment to free trade was the condition of nearly all the wartime loans and aid agreements provided by the United States to Europe. But a liberal world economy, in the last resort, had to be guaranteed by a powerful international state. Free enterprise could create prosperity but it also causes inequality. Prosperity is achieved through rapid change, through the rise and fall of companies, industries and regions; capital tends to flow towards those that are rising and away from those that are falling. Only a strong international state can facilitate the free flow of resources, through providing a recognised international currency, dismantling barriers wherever they are erected, and only such a state can cope with the protest of those who are falling, kindly through aid or harshly through military force. Britain played just such a role in the nineteenth century, through the combination of sterling, the City and gunboat diplomacy. The United States was Britain's obvious successor. A week after Japan surrendered, the US Secretary of State James F. Byrnes made a speech in which he expressed his

> firm conviction that a durable peace cannot be built on an economic foundation of exclusive blocs. . . and economic warfare. . . [A liberal trading system] imposes a special responsibility upon those who occupy a dominant position. . . in world trade. Such is the position of the United States. . .[4]

There were, of course, alternative conceptions of the post-war order. In the same speech, Byrnes referred to the fact that in 'many countries our political and economic creed is in conflict with ideologies which reject both of these principles'.[5] The war had been won by a broad coalition of social and political forces and this has resulted in an enormous growth in the movements of the left, especially in Europe, who conceived the breakdown of the pre-war international system less in terms of an interruption to the smooth workings of the free enterprise system and more in terms of the free enterprise system itself. The political make-up of post-war Europe was entirely different from the Europe of 1939.

> Everywhere [writes Alfred Grosser] the view prevailed that a return to chaotic economic conditions and the social injustice of the pre-

108

war period had to be avoided at all costs. The surprise at the victory of the Labour Party in the July, 1945 British elections can be ascribed to the failure to recognise a profound transnational movement. Everywhere, in France, Denmark, Italy, Germany and Belgium, a push toward the left was taking place. To be 'left' meant to demand social change—which would be brought about by having the national community take charge of the economy. To the extent socialism can be defined, the Europe of 1945-6 was certainly right to call itself socialist.[6]

Any many of the ideas of the socialist parties were shared by the Christian parties which, in several countries, had become the right wing and even by some conservative parties like the Mouvement Republicain Populaire (MRP) in France. Internationally, these ideas were often associated with a 'third force' ideology which envisaged a Europe independent of both the United States and the Soviet Union, of capitalism and communism as practised in the Soviet Union, and in which peace would be preserved at least in part through the activities of the United Nations, and through new genuinely international economic institutions as envisaged by Keynes and others.

To the problems of establishing a liberal international system and of limiting the growth of the left in Europe was added the problem of how to preserve the successful wartime alliance between the state and big business which had served the American economy so well. In particular, the aerospace companies and naval shipyards which had expanded so dramatically during the war, faced, in 1946-7, severe problems of excess capacity and pleaded powerfully for a planned programme of military procurement which would preserve their capacity for mobilisation in case of another war. An initial response to their problems was made in the decision, in 1948, to create a 70 squadron airforce and to expand the navy, before the formation of NATO and the outbreak of the Korean War.

The formation of NATO was the outcome of a complex political process in which relations with the Soviet Union interreacted with internal western politics. As subsequently became clear, it did represent one way of solving these problems. It provided a political framework within which the war-torn European economies could gradually work towards a liberal world economic system. Without NATO, Dean Acheson thought, 'free Europe would split apart'.[7] At that time, the military strength of NATO was not considered significant; the military strength of the West was thought to reside in America's atomic monopoly and there were no plans to augment conventional forces in Europe. After the outbreak of the Korean War, the integrated Command System was established which placed large sections of the European armed forces under the command of an American, the Supreme Allied Commander Europe or SACEUR. The continued monopoly over nuclear weapons justified elaborate procedures of hierarchy and secrecy that confirmed American dominance and were later, particularly in France, to cause considerable resentment. The extension of the principle of NATO to the Far East, through SEATO and ANZUS, to the Middle East, through CENTO, and to Latin America, through the Rio Treaty, during the 1950s, provided an even broader foundation for post-war American authority. It is worth noting that the link between the military alliance and economic relations was often made explicit by the United States, in negotiations over tariffs and troops, military aid and free enterprise, or even in the condition attached in 1968 to the presence of US troops in Germany that West Germany would not convert dollar holdings into gold.

NATO provided a scapegoat, in the form of the Soviet threat, with which to eliminate, over a period of years, alternative political options. Already in the late 1940s the provision of US aid had been used as a form of political pressure, communists having been removed from the French and Italian Governments in 1947. And funds from the CIA, often channelled through the AFL-CIO, had been used to support the activities of Atlanticist factions within the trades unions and the left-wing parties. After Korea, methods became more brutal; McCarthyism was extended to Europe, especially West Germany.

Finally, NATO provided a reason for increased military spending and the preservation of the wartime defence industries. One of the main purposes of military aid to Europe, provided under the 1949 Mutual Defense Assistance

Act, was, according to a memorandum circulating in the US State Department at the time, 'to build up our own military industry'.[8]

For the first two post-war decades, the system worked. The dollar provided a stable international currency. US economic and military aid provided the resources for economic reconstruction, and the dollars which flowed out of the United States returned through the purchase of American goods. Wartime economic controls were gradually dismantled and the United States encouraged the creation of a free trading area through the establishment of the European Community. High military spending stimulated the American economy and was thought to provide technological 'spin-off'. The relaxation of the Cold War, in the early 1960s, the beginnings of detente, all seemed to suggest that this was also a stable political system, capable of securing world peace.

In fact, the situation had begun to change in the 1950s. The rate of economic growth of Western Europe and Japan had become much faster than the American rate of economic growth. American multinationals began to invest abroad, especially in Europe, instead of at home. American military spending became a heavy burden on US economy and society; it absorbed resources that might otherwise have been used for civil investment and innovation, and biassed the American industrial structure in favour of elaborate, expensive and hierarchical types of technology. Americans began to buy more foreign goods and foreigners bought fewer American goods. As the cost of aid and overseas military spending rose, the American balance of payments began to deteriorate, undermining the role of the dollar. America, in effect, was no longer a beneficiary of the liberal world economic system. Resources were flowing, not to America, but to Western Europe and Japan.

From 1965, the rate of economic growth slowed down and, in 1971, the first trade deficit appeared. This was the year, at the time of impending defeat in Vietnam, when the dollar was devalued. America could no longer afford to guarantee the international system. It is this fact, above all others, that explains the present economic and political crisis.

111

The subsequent policies adopted by the Nixon administrations, which included reduction in aid, the withdrawal of troops, various indirect kinds of import restraints, amounted to a kind of parochialism that helped the American economy at the expense of the rest of the world. For instance, it was the end of food aid and the dismantling of grain reserves that was the main cause of the dramatic rise in food prices during the 1970s. The rise in the price of oil can also be explained in this way; the United States can be said to have allowed it to happen because it hurt America less than Europe and Japan and because it benefited American oil companies. In effect, America, itself, became an agent in the erosion of the world economy. It cannot be said that this policy was consciously formulated. Rather, it was a piecemeal response to a variety of special interests affected by the decline of the American economy—farmers, hit by recession and inflation, for instance—and to the broader balance of payments difficulties. The cost of parochialism was borne by foreigners, particularly those located in the slow-growing regions of the world—the economic periphery of Europe—Britain, Ireland, Southern Europe—and by the underdeveloped countries. It gave rise to new forms of conflict and protest and encouraged the development of new centres of power, able to provide wider protection against the vagaries of American power.

The trend to parochialism was opposed, not only by the makers of American foreign policy who had not adjusted to the new conditions of the world, but also by the most powerful sections of American society, the international business community. While American labour, farmers, and domestic American capital may have suffered from America's economic decline, US multinationals continued to benefit from the dynamism of the European and Japanese economies. The Trilateral Commission which informed the thinking of the Carter Administration represented an attempt to re-establish the liberal world order on the basis of power sharing between the United States, Europe, and Japan. But it has proved impossible for an American President to act on behalf of this new internationalism; because it can only be done at domestic American expense. The renewed emphasis on military alliance, the efforts of the Carter Administration to cope with the international problems of money, energy, food or tariffs, turned out to be expensive, in both economic and political terms. The posture of liberal internationalism resulted in a renewed trade deficit, the fall of the dollar and draconian economic measures. The ambivalence of the Carter Administration, its failures, and ultimately its political defeat, all stem from this fundamental dilemma; whether to accept the national costs of being a world power or the international costs, in terms of the break-up of the post-war system, of not being one. The new Reagan Administration represents an undisguised nostalgia for the 1950s when the interests of the United States and capitalist world economy were the same—an attempt to reassert an American dominated global order. It is bound to come unstuck over the cost of defence and economic liberalism; the danger is that this could further encourage an increasing resort to military, as opposed to economic, instruments of power, to repression both at home and abroad—an attempt literally to force a way out of the dilemma.

The decline of America has accompanied the rise of Western Europe. Economic growth has concentrated in West Germany, Belgium, the Netherlands, northeast France and northern Italy. During the 1950s, the United States encouraged the creation of the European Community, as a contribution to a liberal world economy and as a way of minimising the risk of alternative political options which might have still developed in France and Italy. In particular, the United States supported the membership of Britain as a way of widening the free trade area and, it was thought, conferring an additional element of political stability. This conception of Europe was shared by multinational companies as well as those sections of society located in the fast-growing regions of Europe; it might be described as the Atlanticist conception. In practice, of course, the European Community represented a compromise between the Atlanticists, who favoured the creation of the free trade area and, later, the creation of a stable European currency as well as political integration, and another group, which might be termed Gaullist, which reflected the interests of national producers—

farmers, arms companies, etc.— and which viewed the Community as a form of wider protection against the United States. De Gaulle saw British membership of the Community as a threat to Europe and, in more or less abandoning NATO in 1966, he revived some of the 'third force' concepts of the early post-war era. In the community, elements of Gaullism persist in the common external tariff, the common agricultural policy and in the cooperation on high technology projects, particularly armaments.

During the 1950s and 1960s, however, when the post-war American consensus was beginning to break down, a new consensus was developing in Western Europe. The Christian and liberal parties which were largely backed by big business and which, immediately after the war, owed their positions, in large part, to American support adopted, at an early stage, an Atlanticist stance. Gaullism, or even old-fashioned nationalism, remained an element within conservative parties, mainly in France and Britain. The lead of the Christian parties was followed, gradually, by many of the parties of the left. The very success of the post-war system promoted the realignment of European politics. There was a general sense that the world had learned how to manage capitalist crises, and that capitalism, harnessed to a stable international political system and social reform, was relatively humane and successful. In West Germany, for instance, at the Bad Godesberg Convention in 1959, the Social Democrat Party adopted

> an outspokenly revisionist programme which proclaimed the party's attachment to Christianity, the profit motive, and a programme of moderate social reform.[9]

And this approach was, of course, associated with a benign view of the United States as manager of the system. These realignments enabled the Social Democrats to enter government, during the 1960s, in some form or another in every European country, except France and Ireland. During the late 1960s and 1970s, this political realignment affected the Communist Parties as well, through the development of Eurocommunism. In particular, the PCI, in establishing a political stance that was independent of Moscow, relaxed its opposition to NATO as well as to many of the institutions of capitalism, which allowed for the 'historic compromise' with the Christian Democrats.

The economic crisis of the 1970s undermined the new consensus. The sucking of resources from the economic periphery of Europe has drawn attention to the unevenness of economic growth and made more visible its social and political costs—the growth of state power, the centralisation of business, the waste and pollution, the search for capital intensive forms of energy, the excessive expenditure on armaments. These developments have drawn protest not only from farmers, small businessmen and workers in declining regions but from all groups which had been effectively excluded from the political process as it was established after the war; owing to the success of the post-war system, this had not, up to the 1970s, seemed to matter. The protests have been expressed in the rise of movements for regional autonomy (Wales, Scotland and Occitania); in new Poujadist tendencies in certain right-wing and centre parties; in a series of single-issue campaigns about feminism, civil rights, nuclear energy, workers plans and so on; and above all in a new left-ward move at the grass roots of the Socialist and Social Democrat Parties and in the trades unions, a move towards a re-engagement of the left in political and economic life.

The breakdown of consensus is apparent in the defeat of consensus parties—Giscard in France, Callaghan in Britain.

In Britain, for example, the phenomenon of Thatcherism can be seen as a response to the breakdown of consensus. Like Reaganism, it is an attempt to return to the 1950s, to an alliance dominated by a Special Relationship between Britain and the United States, to a combination of successful capitalism and anti-communism. When members of the new British Social Democrat Party talk about a realignment of British politics, what they are in fact talking about is an attempt to save the Atlanticist consensus of the 1950s, in the face of new political forces that have emerged in the periphery of Europe but which, as the crisis deepens, will begin to affect the centre of Europe—Germany, France and Benelux—as well.

The latest and perhaps the most important of the protest movements to have emerged is the disarmament campaign.

115

And this is closely linked to the shifts of opinion within the left-wing parties. It is, of course, the central issue for it is about the future of the NATO alliance and, by implication, about the ways in which we can or cannot solve present economic and political dilemmas. In what follows, I shall try to explain the development of the current debate about nuclear weapons in the context of these wider policital and economic considerations.

THE DEBATE ABOUT NUCLEAR WEAPONS

NATO strategy is based on an enduring myth—the myth of Soviet conventional superiority. We know, from authoritative Western sources, that there is, in fact, a rough conventional balance in Europe. The Soviet Union has marginally more men in Central Europe, although nowhere else, and has many more tanks although these are, to a large extent, offset by NATO's anti-tank forces. During the 1970s, the conventional balance, as measured in quantitative ratios of men, tanks and aircraft, actually moved in NATO's favour.[10] Only by a fantastic stretch of the imagination, which is daily made in NATO headquarters, in the speeches of the politicians, in the media, does the Soviet Union possess sufficient forces for a conventional attack on Western Europe.

But the myth endures. It endures because it is so central to the ritual which surrounds the ownership and control of nuclear weapons. Essentially, the ritual takes the form of an elaborate replay of World War II, in which the Soviet Union plays the role of Nazi Germany charging across the North German plains in a conventional blitzkrieg and in which gallant America, with its superior technology, comes to the rescue of the beleaguered Europeans. Only such a drama, which keeps alive the memory of the American victory in 1945, can justify our readiness to place Europe in thrall to American nuclear weapons. Only recently, the West German defence minister, Herr Apel, said of the growing disarmament movement in West Germany:

> The younger people in our country and in Europe have to some extent never learned the lessons of history. They don't know anything about Hitler.[11]

116

Both because of the inability to take in the awesome implications of nuclear weapons, and because of the way in which the military institutions were organised, the strategy which governed the potential use of nuclear weapons was grafted on to existing strategy. The theory of deterrence was drawn from the experience of strategic bombing. And the language in which the theory was expressed, of numbers and of balances, seemed to imply that nuclear weapons were just bigger and better versions of the weapons of World War II. To those who are not blinkered by the experience of 1945, the young people to whom Apel refers, perhaps, there is an air of total and incomprehensible unreality about the way the debate about nuclear strategy is conducted.

When NATO was formed, the strength of the West, as mentioned earlier, was seen to reside in America's atomic monopoly. Seen from another perspective, it could be said that the cohesion of the West was symbolised in US control over the use of nuclear weapons. After the Soviet Union developed the bomb and an effective means of delivery, the problem of credibility began to be talked about. The problem was expressed in terms of European insecurity, that Europeans might not believe the US would come to the aid of Europe in the event of a Soviet attack for this would result in retaliation against American territory. Kissinger, in his well known speech in Brussels in September 1979, said that US assurances to Europe

> cannot be true, and if my analysis is correct we must face the fact that it is absurd to base the strategy of the West on the credibility of the threat of mutual suicide.[12]

But the problem of credibility could be expressed differently. Once the readiness of the US to engage in nuclear war is questioned, does not this weaken the significance of the possession of nuclear weapons and hence loosen the hold of the alliance system over the political and economic order? This meaning of credibility was more obvious outside Europe where there were real threats to American hegemony, than it was within the NATO alliance. For, by the late 1950s, it was becoming clear that the threat to engage in nuclear war, the memory of World War II, was insufficient to prevent revolutions in Latin America and Asia. When the presence of an atomic howitzer did just manage to stop the Chinese from taking Quemoy and Matsu in 1957, the question inevitably arose: What if it hadn't? The doctrine of flexible response, elaborated by the Kennedy Administration, according to which the US would respond to threats with appropriate responses, was supposed to increase the credibility of American power by making it clear that the United States would engage in conventional as well as nuclear war. The doctrine paved the way for the Vietnam War which drained the American economy and represented a tremendous blow for credibility.

In Europe, the doctrine of flexible response also comprised the idea of tactical or 'limited' nuclear war, although there was never complete trans-Atlantic agreement about what this meant. The official doctrine, known as MC-1413, was described as a

> ladder of escalation options [which] would subsequently exist from conventional to strategic forces, via the nuclear forces deployed in the European theater, both those for tactical use and those longer range systems assigned to SACEUR.[13]

The doctrine was the outcome of a debate in Europe about the sharing of atomic control, which was expressed in the language of credibility. The development of independent nuclear forces in Britain and France can be seen in terms of the persistence of nationalism in these two countries. It was, at least in the case of Britain, an attempt to share the power to engage in nuclear war. But it was justified in terms of credibility, the argument that, in an era of Mutual Assured Destruction, the US would be reluctant to come to Europe's aid in the event of a Soviet threat. Various proposals for power sharing in NATO were put forward, including the MLF proposal, but, in the end, the doctrine of flexible response together with deployment of so-called forward based strategic systems—Poseidon submarines and F-111s assigned to SACEUR—was thought to allay European fears. The argument was that the US would be less reluctant to engage in a 'lower level' option, i.e. conventional, tactical nuclear or even Euro-strategic war, because this would not necessarily involve US territory and that, therefore, US support for Europe would be more convincing. The implication was that the US once more had asserted its power over the alliance because its willingness to engage in nuclear war in Europe, its power over European lives had, once again, become credible.

During the 1970s, this notion hardened. If Vietnam undermined the belief in American conventional military power, then the power of American nuclear weapons had to be reasserted, through a new emphasis on weapons for war fighting as opposed to war deterring. Schlesinger's Counterforce Doctrine and Presidential Directive 59 were all part of this new emphasis. So were the stickers which said 'Nuke the Ayatollah', and the new Vietnam revisionism, according to which the US lost the war, not because it failed to understand the political nature of the war, not because the technology was too sophisticated and capital-intensive, not because there was a breakdown in military authority, but because the US Government was constrained by unpatriotic elements in the media and the universities from using its military power to the full.

It should be noted that this new emphasis is as much theoretical as practical. The United States targeting plans always included military (i.e. tactical) targets, and war planning for Europe always included the option of using battlefield nuclear weapons, which were introduced in Europe as early as 1954. It was rather a change in stated doctrine. Further, as many of the proponents—except perhaps the more extreme Reaganites—have made clear, the new emphasis does not *actually* envisage limited nuclear war. Brown, in his Naval War College speech, expressed the view that limited nuclear war could never remain limited. Rather, it is supposed to enhance deterrence by convincing the Russians that America is more ready to start a limited nuclear war than an all-out strategic, i.e. mutual suicide, nuclear war. Is it supposed to convince the Europeans as well?

Few Europeans ever accepted the American version of flexible response. From the very beginning, battlefield nuclear weapons were envisaged in Europe, as political symbols of the American strategic guarantee. And the ambiguity about their role remained in the differing trans-Atlantic perceptions of the doctrine of flexible response. The increasing emphasis on US credibility and on war fighting was essentially a way of emphasising the American role within alliance. From the late 1960s, it was no longer clear that this was desirable for the Atlanticists in Europe since American power was no longer exercised on behalf of the international community. The Atlanticists in Europe were concerned to preserve the alliance and, at the same time, to prevent it from being abused in the interests of American parochialism. In keeping with the views of the Trilateral Commission, their aim was to develop power sharing within the alliance. Chancellor Schmidt placed great emphasis on 'partnership' and, during the 1970s, Germans were placed in several senior positions in the NATO military hierarchy. In this context, the aim of nuclear strategy was to ensure that Europe and America were 'in it together', that there was no way in which the US could exercise control over European lives without also involving American lives. 'Limited' nuclear war, far from being a way of 'decoupling' the US strategic guarantee, was rather a way of ensuring that the US could not act independently of European interests because such a war would inevitably escalate.

This difference of perspective has been central to the whole debate about cruise and Pershing missiles. The role of nuclear weapons in cementing the alliance is accepted by Atlanticists in both Europe and America. The issue turns on whose behalf the alliance is being cemented. For the Americans, cruise and Pershing represent an additional 'option' between tactical nuclear warfare and all-out nuclear war—a way of further enhancing credibility. It is interesting to note that one of the guidelines of the High Level Group which was established by the NATO Nuclear Planning Group in October 1977 to make proposals for the modernisation of American forward-based systems—so-called Euro-strategic systems—was as follows:

> To satisfy public perceptions concerning the credibility of response, it was considered that the systems should have as much visibility

as possible. Hence, a preference for land-based systems.[14]

Was this to demonstrate to the public the readiness to resist Soviet aggression or the extent of US control over Europe? Certainly, in the event, the concerned public turned out to be much more worried about the latter implication. Likewise, the main advantage of cruise missiles, in contrast to Pershing IIs which are much faster and less vulnerable, was that cruise provided

> the capability of attacking a wider range of targets from several different bases thereby increasing the opportunity for participation among member countries through deployment on their soil.[15]

i.e. further increasing 'political visibility' of American power. That the Americans envisaged the new land-based systems as a way of increasing their readiness to engage in nuclear war in Europe is suggested by the fact that one of the main arguments for cruise and Pershing was the fact that existing forward based systems were

> too closely associated with central strategic systems, a factor which might inhibit an American President from using them.[16]

For the European Atlanticists, the case for cruise and Pershing was precisely the opposite—a way of ensuring that the US strategic systems were closely tied to Europe, that because cruise and Pershing were to be part of the strategic arsenal, the US could not engage in nuclear war in Europe without risking suicide. The argument, of course, as always, was couched in terms of the Soviet threat. It was argued, particularly by Schmidt, that the SALT negotiations had detached American strategic systems from Europe, especially because Soviet Backfire bombers and SS-20s assigned to the European theatre, had been left out of the negotiation. In my view, Schmidt was primarily concerned to tie negotiations on theatre nuclear weapons to the SALT process in order to make more explicit the link between Europe and the strategic guarantee. His IISS lecture of October 1977, which I happened to attend, was more a demand for negotiations on

European theatre nuclear weapons than a demand for new forward based systems. When the decision on cruise and Pershing was taken, the German insistence that these remain exclusively under American control is to be seen as insistence that these systems are part of the US strategic deterrent, and not in any way limited to Europe. Thus, the Atlanticists in Europe support cruise and Pershing as an element of the US strategic deterrent, tend to oppose the existence of battle-field nuclear weapons in Europe, and emphasise the continuation of the SALT process and the inclusion of negotiations on theatre nuclear weapons. This position corresponds to the views of the former liberals in the Carter Administration, the participants and supporters of the Trilateral Commission.

But the cruise issue remains ambiguous. Many members of the Reagan Administration attacked the decision because they believed that cruise and Pershing were not adequate for war fighting; Haig described the decision as the result of 'political expediency and tokenism'. On the other hand, many Europeans fear those very same characteristics that seem to suggest that the US might, in fact, engage in nuclear war. According to Simon Lunn, Director of the North Atlantic Assembly's Military Committee:

> Finally, the LRTNF (long range theatre nuclear forces) moderniza-tion decision constitutes a pragmatic decision between those who believe that European based nuclear forces have a functional war fighting role to play and those who argue that the role is purely to enhance deterrence. The decision, therefore, left unresolved a number of deep-seated issues concerning the appropriate role of nuclear weapons in alliance strategy. It did not satisfy those who believe that to be credible, nuclear weapons should be usable; and it displeased those who regard nuclear weapons as political instruments of deterrence and who believe that the political costs of moderniza-tion far outweigh the gains of military capabilities. This disagree-ment on NATO military strategy is now more likely to become a political debate.[17]

There is, however, no resolution to these issues. For there is no way in which the Atlantic system can be restored in such a way as to act truly in Atlantic and not American interests. As the Americans are squeezed economically and

122

otherwise, the danger is more frequent and more threatening reassertions of American power. The Atlanticist Europeans are caught between two options. They can try to create an alternative European-based international system, linked perhaps with the European community, which would imply, in nuclear terms, the possession of independent European nuclear forces—an alliance with the European Gaullists. Such an option could be dangerously divisive and this may perhaps already be recognised in Atlanticists circles. The alternative is to join with the growing disarmament movement in rejecting nuclear weapons altogether. This is in keeping with anti-militarist sentiments in the two centres of successful capitalism—West Germany and Japan—but it could also open up all kinds of new domestic political shifts which could threaten the basis of the liberal world order. It also raises a whole set of questions for the disarmament movement itself. If indeed the assertion of the right to live necessarily involves a rejection of current relations of power, it is possible to make common cause with those who do not reject but merely favour a shift in current relations of power?

NOTES

1. Alfred Grosser, *The Western Alliance, European-American Relations since 1945* (London: Macmillan, 1980), p. 172.
2. Parts of this section are drawn from my *The Disintegrating West* (London: Penguin Books, 1979).
3. Quoted in David Horowitz, *From Yalta to Vietnam* (London: Penguin Books, 1967), p. 80.
4. Quoted in Walter Lefeber, *America, Russia and the Cold War, 1945-71* (New York: John Wiley & Sons, Inc, 1972), p. 7.
5. Ibid.
6. Grosser, op. cit., p. 52.
7. Lefeber, op. cit., p. 78.
8. Quoted in Lefeber, op. cit., p. 79.
9. *European Political Parties*, P.E.P., George Allen and Unwin, London, 1967, p. 35.
10. See Dan Smith, *Defence of the Realm in the 1980s* (London: Croom Helm, 1980).
11. Quoted in *Washington Star*, 26 March, 1981.
12. See Geoffrey Treverton, 'Global Threats and Trans-Atlantic Allies', *International Security*, Fall 1980.
13. *The Modernization of NATO's long-range Theatre Nuclear Forces*. Report prepared for the Sub Committee on Europe and the Middle East, Committee on Foreign Affairs, US House of Representatives, by the Foreign

Affairs and National Defense Division, Congressional Research Service, Library of Congress, December 31, 1980, Washington D.C. USGPO, 1981, p. 11.
14. Ibid., p. 20.
15. Ibid., p. 23.
16. Ibid., p. 00.
17. Ibid., p. 45.

Part II:

Disarming Europe

NUCLEAR WEAPONS AND EAST-WEST RELATIONS: A SOCIALIST VIEW

István Kende

Europe was the principal theatre of both world wars. For the last 36 years, however, there has been no war between any two countries of Europe. In modern times it is the longest period of peace in Europe. This is a fact of special importance. For all of us, for the whole of mankind, it has become vital not only to prolong this long period of peace, but also to make it permanent and secure. No matter how reassuring it may sound to say that we are now living in the longest period of peace, it is still true that the climate in Europe today is more tense than ever since the Second World War. There has never been such a huge quantity of such powerful weapons, including nuclear weapons, accumulated in Europe.

The countries of Europe belong to two different social systems. According to data of 1978, 51.5 per cent of the continent's population belong to capitalist 'western' and 48.5 per cent to 'eastern' socialist countries. The territorial ratio of Europe, on a similar western-eastern basis, is 34.6 to 65.4 per cent. This division and many other factors, which include the automatism of the military alliances, the direct local confrontation of the world's two largest powers, and the amount of the accumulated weaponry, mean that even the smallest relatively local conflict in Europe—especially a conflict between states of different social systems—would turn immediately into an all-European war: the nature of the two military alliances makes it almost inevitable. And a European war would turn, with equal certainty, into a global war. In addition to these factors, a substantial part of Europe—mainly the western countries—are fundamentally dependent on countries outside Europe from the point of

127

view of economic supply, industrial production and above all the exigencies of the war-like situation.

Peace in Europe does not itself assure peace in the rest of the world, as the history of the last decades has tragically demonstrated. But a war in Europe would inevitably involve other regions of the world. Therefore, anything that decreases tension and the danger of war in Europe, and especially anything that eliminates war from the continent, is in the universal interest of the whole of mankind. Consequently it is desirable to restore the process of detente in Europe, to extend detente to the military field, and to institutionalise confidence-building measures.

One of the most important steps on the road to that goal is the elimination of the greatest danger—the threat of nuclear war in Europe. Today, the 'density' of nuclear weapons in this continent is far greater than anywhere else. Naturally, any step along the road to nuclear disarmament, no matter how concrete or significant it may be, can only decrease and not finally eliminate the danger of war. For today the gap between nuclear and non-nuclear weapons is less distinct; there are and may be more weapons of mass destruction, which though they cannot be classified as nuclear, are not less destructive—the prohibition and elimination of such weapons is, therefore, equally important. On the other hand, a war with conventional weapons may turn into a nuclear war even if certain zones or entire regions were made free of nuclear weapons.

The Warsaw Pact countries are unanimous in their conviction that today the prevention of a world war is one of the most important, or rather *the* most important duty of mankind. Every single step towards reducing the nuclear danger brings us closer to fulfilling that duty. Under current international conditions there is little hope of achieving comprehensive global agreements like general and complete disarmament or the dissolution of both NATO and the Warsaw Pact (even though such dissolution is written into the constitution of the Warsaw Pact). Nor is it likely that the production of nuclear weapons will be prohibited and their stockpiles eliminated or that all-European disarmament agreements covering all sorts of weapons could be achieved.

While all this remains a cherished goal, we must first insist on partial measures, on taking 'small steps'. We must search for the fields where agreements may be reached between the two military alliances, or between certain states within the two groups. We must look for possibilities in that direction and we must guide the mass movements and general demands accordingly. We must reduce tensions in order to create favourable conditions for negotiations, and then for agreements.

The following points are possibilities, tasks and suggestions in that direction:

1. URGENT RATIFICATION OF SALT II

This is not in fact a European issue but a demand for bilateral agreement between the two major powers. Nevertheless, it is not to be considered a purely bilateral and 'extra-European' matter. Every factor which leaves room for confrontation between the two major nuclear powers, carries with it the danger of a conflict in Europe, and not simply the threat of a conflict 'over the heads' of European countries. The assumption that any kind of superpower conflict could occur without involving Europe is even more unrealistic than formerly. Therefore, an agreement on strategic arms limitation between the two major powers must be considered primary, a sort of *conditio sine qua non,* even though SALT II in its original form is no more than a 'ceiling agreement' (which does not really mean any disarmament but provides for further steps in that direction, e.g. SALT III); nevertheless, if seemingly legal but in fact fundamentally political obstacles could be removed, it may prove to be an important political element in the recreation of detente, or at least in a 'break' within the spiralling arms race.

2. PREVENTION OF ANY FURTHER ESCALATION

It is necessary to demand or support every sort of moratorium and to urge such agreements immediately without reservations. This should be done even if the moratorium were to be provisional or conditional on the start or conclusion of negotiations.

A moratorium may be suggested, for example, in the

following fields:
a) The cessation or suspension of all nuclear tests by members of the two military alliances. This of course, is not really a European question but, like SALT, is inseparable from the sphere of European security.
b) Freezing the military budgets of the European states or of members of the two military alliances—that is, a ban on their increase, or as a further step, their decrease by mutual agreement.
c) Freezing the membership of the existing military alliances, of their sphere of activity, etc.
d) An undertaking by the states in question not to research, produce or deploy new weapons of mass destruction, nor to create new weapon systems.
e) The quantitative and qualitative freezing of all nuclear deployments in Europe, and first of all, freezing the deployment of medium-range missiles. These involve a particular danger for Europe, because despite their medium range, they directly threaten certain areas around Europe in North Africa and West Asia. Such agreements would of course apply to all weapons in this group (cruise missiles, SS series, Pershings, etc.).

3. FURTHER NEGOTIATIONS

Making use of the period of grace created by such measures of moratorium, or even without such measures, negotiations *must be initiated* between the relevant powers with one or more of the following aims:
a) With the participation of all the European states or all states which are members of the military alliances, *an all-European conference on disarmament* should be called for the purpose of investigating and exploring even the slightest possibilities of agreement on any measures of limitation. At such a conference or within the framework of any other negotiations, agreements could be reached either on the questions mentioned in paragraph 2 above or on any further questions, for example:
b) The prohibition or cessation of the production of nuclear weapons, their spread in Europe (or over a wider area), and of the deployment and planned increase of such weapons.

This should be followed by a provision made for dismantling previous deployments, and decreasing and eliminating stockpiles.

c) The total prohibition of the production and deployment in Europe (or over a wider area) of any new weapons of mass destruction including conventional, nuclear, neutron or any new type.

d) A review of the effectiveness and realisation of confidence-building measures already in practice, with a view to deepening or restoring confidence, and extending such measures to cover the whole of Europe, as suggested by France in Madrid, 'from the Atlantic to the Urals'.

In this context, it is necessary to look more closely at the question of confidence. Confidence is a matter of political climate. So-called confidence-building measures, like those embodied in the Final Act of the Helsinki conference in 1975 must be considered very significant politically despite their limited military importance. When viewed in a broader perspective, lack of confidence would undoubtedly prompt military decisions which in turn promote escalation. Ultimately, such military decisions are, of course, the consequences of political decisions. Thus by way of military decisions, mistrust further accumulates in the political atmosphere and the result is both military and political escalation. For example, the deployment of new weapon systems and the sudden increase in military budgets are acts of military escalation but they are political decisions. They increase the arms race and deepen mistrust. Conversely, discontinuing—even temporarily—any measure of military escalation is in itself a political act which can build confidence. And such an act is badly needed in today's tense Europe. If leaders of confronting states were to meet on a high, or even better, a summit level, events could be pointed in the right direction and thereby also build confidence.

4. NUCLEAR-WEAPON-FREE ZONES

It is necessary to consider the possibility of turning certain parts of Europe into nuclear-weapon-free zones which are free from all kinds of missiles deployed there. There may be several approaches. One point of departure may be the zone of central Europe proposed in the 1957 Rapacki plan; another one may be the idea of turning the Mediterranean into a peace zone. Such zones may gradually lead to turning the whole of Europe into a peace zone. The concrete meaning of the idea ought to be defined through negotiations.

It would be desirable to initiate parallel negotiations with respect to other regions as well—like the Indian Ocean, the Middle East and the Far East, Africa or certain parts of it, and the Gulf area including Afghanistan. It would be worth starting talks among the parties involved in all these regions. Turning one region into a peace zone would evidently improve the situation in other regions which would encourage setting up such zones in Europe, and vice versa.

Conflicts in any region create difficulties for peace and security in other regions. The socialist countries, however, are firmly convinced—just as they were in periods of the gravest regional conflicts, as during the war in Indochina—that every political agreement, even on a regional level, promotes a general willingness to reach agreements, improves the atmosphere of international negotiations and contributes to the settlement of other conflicts. The interrelationship of regions entails not only the danger of spreading tensions and conflicts, but also the possibility of spreading detente. There is, in addition, the possibility of transplanting favourable settlements from one area to another. When all parties honestly search for a solution, then any single reinforcement of peace, and any improvement in the climate of tensions, will have beneficial effects on other regions.

5. NO-FIRST-USE PLEDGE
All states, members of NATO and the Warsaw Pact, as well as all the non-aligned and neutral states of Europe should undertake to renounce the first use of weapons, nuclear and conventional, either in Europe or from Europe or aimed at Europe.

6. INTERNATIONAL PRESSURE
It would be a good idea to establish international committees or to convene international gatherings (with a European or global sphere of action) with the participation of outstanding

scientists, public figures, artists and experts. These should also include representatives of various movements and conferences dealing with European or world security, such as the Pugwash Movement or its European national committees, the European peace movements, the Amsterdam research conference on nuclear disarmament in Europe, and so on. The task of such forums would be to provide effective arguments which reveal the dangers of a nuclear catastrophe, to demonstrate the vital importance of averting such dangers, to publish analyses and appeals, and to make data available as well as arguments and articles prepared either by themselves or by other institutions such as peace research institutes. It would also be wise to convene periodic, perhaps annual, 'summit meetings' of the leading officials of various organisations with a view to coordinating the basic principles and main tasks. Or, a permanently operative liaison committee could be set up. There may be many other possibilities. All this would by no means limit the activities of the various movements already in existence. On the contrary, they would be supplied with information and arguments. If Europe should fail to take these steps, or other appropriate steps, if the European masses are not roused against the spiralling arms race, the increasing nuclear danger and unceasing escalation, then the danger will simply increase further. Every move will inevitably cause counter-moves, every escalation on one side is bound to provoke a similar response on the other side.

To fight against all this is a duty of primary importance. It is a duty which is in the vital interests of Europe and of the whole of mankind.

FOR A NORDIC NUCLEAR-WEAPON-FREE ZONE

Erik Alfsen

1. ARGUMENTS AGAINST AND FOR A NORDIC NUCLEAR-WEAPON-FREE ZONE

My point of departure will be the final document of the United Nations Special Session on Disarmament in 1978. The concept of a 'nuclear-weapon-free zone' is elucidated in paragraphs 60-62, and it is recommended that such zones be established.

A nuclear-weapon-free zone is, basically, a limited area which, by virtue of a treaty, is declared free of nuclear weapons. Within this zone, member states or their allies shall not produce, store or employ any form of nuclear weapons. Moreover, the nuclear powers shall renounce the right to use nuclear weapons against countries within the zone.

Until recently, the mere intimation that the Nordic countries should establish a nuclear-weapon-free zone has been taboo and has been received with all the irrational aversion typically reserved for taboo images. The arguments against a nuclear-weapon-free zone went as follows:

First, it is detrimental to establish a nuclear-weapon-free zone in the North. In reality, it would mean a unilateral policy of relinquishment because the adversary would have all the advantages stemming from such an agreement.

Second, it is naive to believe in agreements and guarantees. When war breaks out, the adversary will violate the zone agreement.

Third, the Nordic countries *are* already a nuclear-weapon-free zone.

135

Obviously, these arguments are inconsistent and I would like to make the following comments:

First, the creation of a nuclear-free Nordic zone will not be a unilateral undertaking. The Nordic countries consist not only of the NATO countries Norway and Denmark, but also of the non-aligned Sweden and the neutral Finland which has signed a treaty of Friendship, Cooperation and Mutual Assistance with the Soviet Union. This means that in the event of a superpower conflict, both parties would have to renounce the right to use nuclear weapons in areas which they conceive of as being part of their own security system. And it may be worth mentioning that it is the superpowers, the USA and the Soviet Union, which must renounce a right, not Nordic countries like Norway and Finland. It may be a rational defence policy for a superpower to fight a limited nuclear war on another nation's land. But a nuclear war on one's own territory would be the direct opposite of defence for the front line countries. It would mean destruction of everything that should be defended. Therefore it is in our own interest that we wish to eliminate the possibility of nuclear weapon use in the Nordic countries.

Second, we must remember that modern war is prepared in peacetime. These preparations are concrete and, to a large extent, verifiable. The zone agreement can be applied, then, to limit such preparations. And on the whole, international agreements are respected in time of peace. Therefore, I emphasise the effects a zone agreement will have in peacetime. It will be a step in the effort to halt nuclear armaments, to contribute to detente between the power blocs and to prepare the way for further actions which can build up confidence. The major purpose of the nuclear-weapon-free zone agreement, as with all good security policies, is to *prevent* war.

Third, it is not correct that the Nordic countries already form a nuclear-weapon-free zone as this concept has been defined. No binding agreement has been made. On our side, we are free to abolish our self-imposed restrictions, and none

136

of the nuclear powers has renounced the right to use nuclear weapons against the Nordic countries.

2. THE FOUR PILLARS OF A NWFZ·

After this short review of the most common arguments, I would like to examine what a zone plan actually involves. I will be very brief. It is much too early to present anything resembling a draft treaty at the present time.

I would like to base the discussion on some principles which Ambassador Jens Evensen calls 'the four main pillars'. The first two concern the guarantees. They include two types. The zone countries guarantee that they will remain free of nuclear weapons. On the other hand, the nuclear powers guarantee that they will not use nuclear weapons against countries in the zone. Thirdly, in conjunction with the zone agreement, a control apparatus has to be created to see that the agreement is observed. These three principles are juridical. The fourth principle—and possibly the most important one—is political. The creation of nuclear-weapon-free zones can contribute to the relaxation of tension which is necessary to preserve peace in a tense international situation. The important concepts here are: *bilateral guarantees, control* and *detente.*

In addition to these general points, more specific factors are also involved. First, I would mention that a zone agreement can include additional accords, so-called collateral agreements. These can comprehend weapons systems or installations which are found within the zone and which do not contain nuclear warheads, but which are nevertheless of importance for a nuclear war. They can also encompass weapon systems which are found outside of the zone, and which are either aimed at the zone or will violate the zone's airspace. In this connection, I would like to point out that I prefer collateral agreements which are selective and take into account the nature of the weapon systems and not only their location.

Nuclear-weapon-free zones in Europe will, more so than in other parts of the world, take on the characteristics of buffer zones between the power blocs where it will be crucial to reduce tension and develop confidence-building measures.

These zones should include countries on both sides of the dividing line, and they can include non-aligned countries. In the initial phase, we should not try to incorporate parts of the superpowers' own land area, nor areas which are specially important for the strategic balance between them. If one attempts this, one gets involved in all the great and difficult problems which have effectively blocked most disarmament conferences through the years. The idea is to make new openings and launch action in areas which allow for progress, e.g. in areas where nuclear weapons are not found today.

3. THE SPECIFIC PROBLEMS OF A NORDIC NUCLEAR-FREE ZONE

During zonal negotiations, the content of nuclear-weapon-free status must be well defined. Even the concept *nuclear weapon* must be defined more precisely. What about the means of delivery—should they be included? In general, they are not, but it is evident that they must be incorporated in this agreement either by extending the concept of nuclear weapons or by appending a special protocol to the agreement. The questions of *transit* and *air passage* must also be taken up. These concepts are not clearly defined. But generally, transit refers to the transport of nuclear weapons through the zone from one place outside the zone for stationing in another place outside the zone. Air passage means that nuclear weapons are carried by air mobile vehicles, e.g. aircraft, or cruise missiles, through the zone's airspace on their way to a target outside the zone. I think that one should effectively prohibit air passage and adopt restrictive rules concerning transit, prohibiting it totally if possible. It is too early in the game to go into details, but we should be aware of the fact that these problems exist.

Moreover, it is of great importance that the agreements are reasonably balanced. The different elements on each side must be of the same nature. By this I do not refer to a close comparison of weapon systems, but rather to principles: paper guarantees—statements of intent—can be weighed against each other; the same applies to operational restrictions or non-deployment of proposed systems, and also to withdrawal of existing ones. But we must not present such

138

unreasonable demands as a physical withdrawal as compensation for a paper guarantee. One must be somewhat realistic.

As for the delimitation of a Nordic nuclear-weapon-free zone, I feel that the zone area should encompass the continental Nordic countries, where there are no nuclear weapons today, i.e. Denmark, Sweden, Finland and Norway. To me it seems absurd to suggest that the Kola Peninsula, with its strategic weapons directed at the USA should also be included. And I believe that essentially everyone who has thought about the question is aware of this. Initially, one should probably also leave out Iceland. Though ethnically and culturally a part of Scandinavia, Iceland is strategically a part of the North Atlantic area. Even if the Americans do not have nuclear weapons there at present, I would assume that Iceland constitutes such an important part of the American security system that it would complicate zonal negotiations substantially if one were to include this country from the start. The delimitations at sea must be negotiated. I would think that it would be unreasonable to try to use the 200 mile economic zone as a point of departure and that one should begin with traditional 4 or 12 mile limits outside the base-line. But it is obvious that one can have selective collateral agreements for systems farther out in the ocean.

The Baltic Sea presents a special problem. The Swedes have a particular interest in this area and it is possible that a special arrangement could be agreed upon. In the East, the Baltic Sea has been called 'sea of peace' for over 20 years, so we should be able to take them up on this. For many reasons, however, it can be difficult to draw the Baltic Sea into the zone; among other things, the transit problem can be difficult. A possible solution, therefore, might be a collateral agreement which expressly prohibits the weapon system which the Swedes are most concerned about, e.g. the Golf submarines. At any rate, this will have to be the subject of negotiations.

4. A FLEXIBLE PLAN OF ACTION

I would like to stress the fact that during zonal negotiations, one should have a plan of action which does not presuppose that one is going to solve in advance the great and difficult problems of Central Europe—problems which have effectively blocked earlier disarmament initiatives. As to the balance of power in Europe, I feel that it is unfortunate that NATO has become much too dependent on nuclear weapons and that tactical weapons in West Germany play such a decisive role in our defence. This makes it difficult to arrive at actual prohibitions in this area, on a short term basis. Therefore, we should not start with these problems. I see negotiations for a Nordic zone agreement as a first step in a process. Later, the agreement can be extended to a larger European system.

Finally, I would like to touch upon the question of physical reduction or withdrawal of tactical and intermediate range nuclear systems on the Kola Peninsula. It is obviously in our interest to reduce them. The question of what to consider reasonable compensation must be discussed in more detail. It has been pointed out that in the Nordic area there are no western nuclear weapons of parallel importance. But this is not completely true. If we take into consideration the oceans, then we find many western muclear weapons, i.e. on board of aircraft carriers and submarines. Most important in this connection are the new cruise missiles which will be introduced in the near future. There are over 150 large B-52 bombers which are going to be adapted to carry 20 cruise missiles each—altogether a capacity of over 3000 cruise missiles. (This is the limit set by SALT.) This programme will now be speeded up. The first cruise missile planes are to be operative in the winter 1981-82. It is evident that some of these will fly over the North Atlantic and the Norwegian Sea. This can have a destabilising effect and will present serious problems for our Nordic neighbours, Sweden and Finland. Particularly Finland's neutral status will depend upon whether the Finns can convince the Soviet Union that they are willing and, to a reasonable extent, also able to assure that their airspace is not violated. To guard against air passage of cruise missiles is a tremendously difficult problem. Sweden has an advanced radar warning system which the Swedes are deservedly proud of. But they have no early warming systems to detect cruise missiles, and the Swedes are now discussing how to solve this problem. Obviously, they can build a dense network of new radar stations and even introduce airborne radar, but this would be very expensive. The Finns, on their side, should be prepared to meet a certain amount of pressure to promptly detect and alert possible penetration of these cruise missiles, in cooperation with their eastern neighbours.

To practise some restraint in the use of air launched cruise missiles would have a stabilising effect. One could imagine possible ways of limiting the areas where cruise missile planes could cooperate, e.g. in the same way as the Norwegian model of the 24th degree of longitude is applied to allied planes over Norway. One could imagine that something comparable would be a reasonable counterpart during negotiations on certain systems on the Russian side. I mention this to draw attention to the fact that possibilities exist which ought to be examined more closely in the future.

WESTERN EUROPEAN NEUTRALISM*

Ulrich Albrecht

In many Western European countries, and particularly in West Germany, opponents of established defence strategies are looking for an alternative to the dilemmas of current postures: Western Europe cannot be defended with nuclear weapons in actual warfare ('defence dilemma'), and the concept of deterrence by nuclear weapons threatens to destroy exactly what is to be preserved ('deterrence dilemma'). The Europeans have an interest in survival. Therefore, they would react to an emergency in a way which would contradict American policy. Leading US politicians warn against European pacifism or semi-neutralism; this contribution tries to identify and to elaborate the postures which have thus been attacked.

The alternative defence concept is variously labelled 'neutralisation', 'disengagement', or 'nuclear-free zone'. The aim is to diminish the direct confrontation of forces along the line of division of Europe through partial withdrawals of certain military units. The actual policies of European States would be brought more in line with national interests, as a result of new political developments.

The purpose of this contribution is not to describe a new, more sophisticated version of the older proposals. It is rather an effort to defend the basic concept against current lines of thinking in security politics, the state of the arms race, and political reaction. A 'decoupling' from the deterrence systems

*This paper is part of a larger manuscript about current military politics of NATO and the alternatives, written and discussed by a group of German scholars (Wolf-Dieter Narr, who was responsible for this initiative, and Andreas Buro, Egbert Jahn, Ekkehart Krippendorff, plus a number of concerned critics). I contributed the argument about disengagement and neutralism to this collective effort. The responsibility for the text is solely mine, but I profited much from criticism of an earlier draft of this contribution.

could offer more today than ever before. Neutralism provides a concept of detente, which goes well beyond the so-called 'two pillar strategy', the safeguarding of external security in Europe both by an arms build-up *and* detente. Historically one consequence of military de-escalation has been the withdrawal from lines of confrontation, as the Egypt-Israeli accord in the Sinai demonstrates so well.

DISENGAGEMENT, THE INTERMEDIATE STEP

Disengagement is the least radical alternative to current policies; it requires a reorientation of the policies of the two military alliances, but it does not imply the dissolution or even much reshaping of the two blocs. George Kennan introduced the term into the political vernacular in 1957,[1] and the concept was always apparently tied to the political make-up of Europe. Instead of the continued military confrontation of the US and the USSR in Central Europe, Kennan called for the creation of 'reduced' and controlled zones of military effort, maybe even nuclear-free areas.

In the fifties, there was a wide range of disengagement concepts. Anthony Eden, then British Foreign Secretary, put forward a plan for a demilitarised zone at the Berlin conference of ministers of foreign affairs on 29th January, 1954, and at the Geneva Summit of 18th July, 1955: the victorious powers would withdraw their armed forces from all zones of occupied Germany and a German government should be free to seek a coalition with other states.[2] Eden's main domestic opponent, Hugh Gaitskell, leader of Her Majesty's opposition, proposed several improvements to the Eden Plan. He suggested that West Germany, East Germany, Czechoslovakia, Poland and Hungary should quit the two Pacts, all foreign troops should be withdrawn, and the security of the Central European Area should be guaranteed by the four Allied powers.[3] At the same time, Kennan speculated about German reunification: the new Germany 'would function as a neutral factor, which lessens the sharp divide of the two poles in Europe and helps, in the end, to reduce the vigour of conflict between East and West'.[4] Kennan stressed that the stationing of nuclear weapons in West Germany prevented the Soviet Union from seriously

144

considering withdrawing troops to the East.

Similar concepts existed in the East. This approach was accepted in the Soviet Union only after the West German entry into NATO—apparently, disengagement is, in the Soviet perspective, rather a minimum position. The issue of nuclear weapons always occupied a central place in Soviet disengagement concepts. In March 1956, A. Gromyko, then Soviet representative to the UN disarmament negotiations, submitted a plan 'to create in Europe a zone of arms control and inspection, which comprises the territory of both parts of Germany and neighbouring states'. In addition, 'the stationing of military units equipped with nuclear weapons and the storing of atom and hydrogen weapons of any kind shall be forbidden in this zone'.[5] Subsequently, there were repeated Soviet proposals of this nature. However, a Polish proposal received much more publicity. In October 1957, Poland's Foreign Minister Rapacki suggested a prohibition against the storage of nuclear weapons on the soil of both German states and Poland, and the government of the USSR rapidly supported the proposal.[6]

Given that the Scandinavian NATO members have renounced the storage of nuclear weapons unilaterally, it is not unrealistic to envisage a zone of nuclear-free territory across Europe: it would include the nuclear-free north and the nuclear-free south (Austria, Switzerland, Yugoslavia) and would thus comprise an area of diminished armaments between East and West, running through the heart of the continent.

As well as these international initiatives, a large number of proposals were put forward in West Germany. These came from both the SPD and the bourgeois parties. The best known proposal was that of the liberal politician (and member of the Federal Diet) Karl-Georg Pfleiderer, who later became first German Ambassador to Yugoslavia. He suggested that the occupation powers should withdraw to the easternmost and westernmost parts of Germany, so that central Germany, together with Berlin, should become a demilitarised state. The last of these contributions to the German debate was by the SPD-launched 'Deutschland-Plan' in March 1959, which proposed a militarily thinned-out zone in Central Europe, outside both NATO and the Warsaw Pact. Such proposals rarely gained broad political support; during this period, all parties represented in the Federal Diet got rid of their neutralist dissidents largely through expulsion.[7]

Even the narrowest denuclearised 'hose' or stretch of land running from North to South through Central Europe would shatter current bloc politics, not only in bloc-to-bloc relations, but more importantly within the blocs. NATO, today far from being a homogenous entity, is better described as a bunch of divergent groups of members. A central European disengagement would result in significant shifts in the relative importance of these groups. West Germany and any adherent to the concept of a nuclear-free zone would join the category currently comprising the Scandinavian NATO members who do not tolerate nuclear weapons on their soil in peacetime. This would increase the role of the tripartite alliance leadership of nuclear powers, the US, Britain and France. These political shifts, however, would be offset by the advantages for the denuclearised region: in the event of hostilities, this area would serve as a passage of troops rather than as the decisive battleground and the prospects for survival of the territory concerned would be greatly enhanced.

Opponents of the concept stress that the withdrawal of West Germany from NATO would remove the cornerstone of the alliance on the continent. This is certainly true, but NATO in its present form has no stable future either. Whether or not NATO can face up to the challenge of the disengagement option, or a nuclear-free zone, the fragile alliance is going to have to adapt to internal changes. Disengagement is much more realistic than the current political set-up. NATO would no longer be treated as the ideal, closely integrated, cooperative bloc, but rather as the unhomogenous, mutually suspicious, diverging collection of powers that it really is.

In political terms, the most important consequence would be a lessening of the American grip on European politics. With respect to detente policies, such a move would be logical: a certain amount of dissociation is in keeping with the rationale of detente concepts. To put it another way: disengagement would mean a further reshuffling in the relations between Europe and the US, which began with the

'Ostpolitik' of the West German social-liberal coalition. Whether domestic German opinion is willing to acknowledge the fact or not, one important consequence of the recent arrangements negotiated with the USSR and her allies was a qualitative change in the relationship with the US. The new ties with the East gained in relative importance and lead to new perceptions of national interest which often contradicted American perceptions of security priorities. In the event, not only the objectives, but also the ways of pursuing security tend to differ between the US and some of its European allies.

The disengagement idea gained considerable momentum, somewhat to the surprise even of its proponents,[8] after the appeal for a nuclear-free zone 'from Portugal to Poland' was launched in April 1980. The geographical reach of the proposal was, as Mary Kaldor has candidly argued,[9] not so much due to the alliteration of these names, but to the conviction that this concept addresses 'political Europe' which tries to articulate its own future interests. (A slogan ending '. . . to the Urals' would provoke, it was felt, too many negative associations, and raise too many questions about how Soviet politics could come to grips with this differentiation of the Eastern super-power from the United States.)

MAIN ELEMENTS OF THE RECENT DISENGAGEMENT SCHEME
Disengagement could consist of two approaches. One is the reduction of armaments in a given area; the other is the elimination of certain categories of armaments, most notably nuclear weapons. It is hardly conceivable to imagine disengagement in Europe which omits the forward based nuclear systems on both sides; all past proposals for disengagement focused on these weapons.

(a) The nuclear-free zone
There are a number of nuclear-free areas which still exist around the globe. The globalisation of nuclear weapons has not yet occurred. Some areas adhere to formal treaties in this respect, or formal declarations (Latin America), others are effectively nuclear-free (e.g. Africa). It is assumed that

most Eastern European countries are in general also free from Soviet nuclear weapons, and that such weapons are only brought into the region during manoeuvres. Thirdly there is a category of states who do not accept nuclear weapons on their soil in peacetime, e.g. the Scandinavian members of NATO.

This proposal would envisage a formal zone in clearly defined areas of Europe in which there would be no nuclear weapons, and this would be guaranteed by international agreement. The somewhat weaker position of excluding atomic weapons in peacetime cannot apparently be enforced.

To be meaningful, the abolition of these weapons must be complete and exhaustive. There should be no preapred sites for the possible storage of nuclear weapons in case of an emergency, nor should there be installations to facilitate the special communication and deployment guidance required for such arms. A renunciation of nuclear weapons which solely bans the warheads, but accepts the delivery vehicles, storage preparations and means of controlling the possible use of such weapons (as Norway and Denmark do) would have little credibility. The political objective in a nuclear-free zone is that there should be no atomic warfare, and this objective should be made plain publicly.

(b) Other arms reductions

In a zone of disengagement, there are further possibilities for reducing military efforts, beyond the abolition or drastic reduction of nuclear arms. Such measures could deal in particular with the offensive elements in current defence postures. This could mean the heavily armoured shock divisions, e.g. the nine Soviet tank divisions in East Germany, which pose a deeply felt threat to West German security. The measure should be symmetrical, and the Federal Armed Forces also should withdraw their 69 tank battalions from the lines of confrontation. This withdrawal could go beyond the respective national borders of both German states—if other alliance members keep some of their forces on German soil, in the East and in the West, then it should not be possible to envisage a reversed situation.

THE ADVANTAGES OF THE DISENGAGEMENT SCHEME

The most important function of the proposal is that the two antagonist great powers are offered a balanced way of improving their mutual security interests outside their own territories. Non-military forms of security policies should be strengthened, and an experiment towards more significant arms reductions could be carried out.

European states would also profit. Disengagement represents an important countervailing move against the current trends towards a Europeanisation of deterrence, i.e. the idea of war fighting options in the European theatre of war. The prospect of conventional war still remains terrible, but a disengagement zone would represent a measure of reconciliation and would also reduce the danger of a conventional war.

The militarily thinned-out zone would not leave the area without any defence. The ultimate protection by the alliance would remain in force, as long as the zone forms part of the blocs. The true objective of this proposal would, as must be stressed, be the lowering of the risk of a situation where a nuclear umbrella could be needed, in the hope of moving towards a future in which the risk will be zero.

The economic benefits are also worth mentioning. The strain on resources, fiscal bottlenecks, overspending of various kinds would be reduced if a country in a zone of reduced military effort opts out of the arms race. The investment can go into other profitable areas, or in the budget to fight unemployment.

DISENGAGEMENT AND NEUTRALISM

The disengagement project may lead to a neutralist option, depending on whether a zone of disengagement remains stable. Thinking in political terms, however, it is reasonable to consider disengagement as a temporary rather than permanent state. The move towards disengagement would set free forces which would tend to undermine alliance cohesion (and this can be considered as a positive asset), and to dynamise European politics. If West Germany were to opt for the abolition of nuclear weapons in peacetime, like the Scandinavian NATO member states, the role of NATO in Europe as the bearer of deterrence strategies would be considerably diminished: the nuclear role would be confined in peacetime, to the rearward and Southern European powers. Hence disengagement would launch a movement towards the reshaping of NATO (while the Warsaw Pact would be much less affected, given the central role of the USSR). This impact is not an argument against the proposal. The alliance has been facing a series of crises because of its failure to adapt to changing circumstances. It is necessary, however, for the proponents to indicate the reshaping movement. Neutralism is the obvious answer; it is necessarily the basic orientation of the inhabitants of a disengaged area.

The principal difference between disengagement and neutralism can be found in the intra-bloc relationships. Disengagement would be an alternative to the policies pursued both by NATO and the Warsaw Pact, but the alliances themselves would not change much, and would remain basically untouched. In contrast, neutralism aims at the diminution, if not dissolution, of the post-war alliances in Europe.

THE NEUTRALIST OPTION

A declaration to opt out of the arms race of the great powers and to become neutral remains the sole sovereign decision European states can make. European consent to a US decision to authorise field commanders to use nuclear weapons, or in the East support for the equivalent decision by the Soviet leadership, is hardly an expression of sovereignty.

Neutralism may be important in case of war (and has always been studied in this context), but today the concept also offers many attractions for peacetime foreign and security policies. The permanent state of 'non-war' has now become an emergency, for which new solutions are desperately required.

The experts generally argue that[10] the neutral state is obliged to defend its neutrality in case of war. In the past this claim led to predominantly military types of security policies (a neutral power has to organise an independent armament base in order to defend against any threat to its 'armed neutrality'; a neutral power has to deny its territory to foreign troops and it has to remain outside alliances). Today it is important to reconsider the general premises of a neutral-ist posture in peacetime. It is more important now for a neutral power in order to promote its own security, to try to achieve international reconciliation, to promote detente between the alliances, and to encourage arms reductions—all essential objectives in the process of de-escalating the 'non-war' state of affairs characterised by feverish arms races.

The fact that this would lead to a depolarisation of the international security system is not an argument against neutralism. Current strategies based on the balance of power have failed to establish a 'pax sovietica-americana'—the hopes which the two nuclear superpowers placed in a security system, balanced and contained by them, have been definite-ly frustrated. The international system remains prone to conflict, including armed conflict, and the decisive criterion for political power is a state's perceived ability to wage a future war. Confronted with today's methods of conflict resolution, neutralism is an obvious choice for medium and smaller powers, and it would also allow some reduction in armaments.

Neutralism is not the same as neutrality, as it is defined by a number of European states:

(a) *The Swiss concept of neutrality*, which has, in practice, operated since the 16th century, was established *de jure* in 1815. The 'integral' neutrality pursued by this country released the Swiss from participation in military sanctions agreed upon by the League of Nations (since 1920) and also more recently (since 1938) from participation in economic sanctions. Because of the way in which the concept of neutrality is interpreted, Switzerland did not join the UN and did not become a member of the Council of Europe until 1963. Membership in the EEC is not considered compatible with the basic foreign policy principle of this state.

The Swiss stress that their neutrality should remain armed. The range of military options for this end entails the possi-bility of low-level violence tactics, the militia and—at the other end of the spectrum—protection by nuclear weapons (which has actually been demanded).

151

For larger European states, the strict concept of Swiss neutrality offers little attraction. In particular it remains open to question whether significant arms reductions are possible within such a framework. Neutralism in contrast to neutrality (of a single state) can be envisaged as a collective attitude by a group of countries, which might continue to regard their defence efforts as a collective task. NATO and the Warsaw Pact have undertaken such collective efforts in the past; these may be superior to individual measures of defence and may have helped to contain local arms races (e.g. between Greece and Turkey).

(b) Swedish neutrality is, in contrast, to the Swiss concept, little more than a political objective, which has never been fixed by international treaty or domestic legislation. Despite adherence to the posture of 'armed neutrality', Sweden had to make concessions to the Germans in World War II (transportation of war material through the country, the passage of German troops from Norway to Finland, repeated holiday train passages for German troops). During the Finnish-Soviet war, Sweden supported Finland.

The neutralism option proposed here comes close to the Swedish model: the lack of formal organisation for such a policy may indicate a weakness of this position.

(c) The policy of non-alignment, as adopted in Europe by Yugoslavia, is actually a renewed version of an older concept, dating back to Leon Blum's vision of Europe as a 'third force'. The non-aligned countries 'are not organised in blocs, also not in their own bloc, but they remain engaged as far as their moral basis is concerned' (Tito, 1961). The neutralism of the non-aligned powers is not rooted in avoidance of war, but in the motives and objectives of their foreign policies. These are the principles of peaceful co-existence, support for disarmament and detente, recognition of the territorial integrity of each state, and particularly in the Third World, anti-colonialism.

The military politics of the non-aligned countries differ greatly. A number of them were engaged in wars after the formal declaration of these principles. The more industrialised countries in the non-aligned world place considerable emphasis upon defence (in Yugoslavia, men can be drafted for military service from 14 to 68 years of age; women are eligible for auxiliary services until they are 60).

The concept of non-alignment has been primarily adopted by Third World countries. It is based on their development problems and is hence differently applied in these countries. The international context of industrialised countries is different, both in relationship to other industrialised countries and vis à vis the Third World. Neutralism in the 'Northern tier' has to be clearly distinguished from the security demands and the relationships between the two big military alliances of industrialised countries.

HISTORICAL PRECEDENTS

After 1945, there have been several movements towards a neutralisation of parts of central Europe, which will be briefly reviewed here. One of the various US post-war concepts, in vogue in the winter of 1945/46, was the idea of the demilitarisation and neutralisation of Germany on the basis of a 25-year agreement among the four victorious powers (Secretary of State Byrnes was involved in this project).[11] In the spring of 1953, shortly before the Geneva Summit, President Eisenhower and Secretary of State Dulles speculated about whether one could design in Europe a 'neutral security belt' including Germany (this led Chancellor Adenauer to call back his ambassadors in the Western capitals).

There were similar concepts in the East. From the autumn of 1950 (not later; most observers wrongly suggest that March 1952 with Stalin's well-known note was the beginning of these moves) the Soviet leadership became interested in the neutralisation of Germany, at first linked to demilitarisation; later (after 1952) they were willing to concede the possession of 'national' armed forces. When West Germany joined the Western alliance, Soviet diplomacy continued to propose such concepts. The idea was reformulated and narrowed down to the proposal for a nuclear arms-free Europe.

As opinion polls show, neutralism is again a political option capable of mobilising wide support. In August 1980, a poll showed that 43 per cent of the West Germans asked backed a neutralist position between the two great powers (and a majority of SPD supporters polled favoured neutralism).[12] In letters to newspaper editors, recently, specific proposals have been submitted (e.g. the creation of a 'new neutralist *Sperriegel* across Europe', comprising France, Germany, Switzerland, Austria and Sweden). In 1945 the 'reputation of neutralism was at its lowest possible point' (Riklin). Since then, a new respect for neutralism has gradually developed. In 1953 neutral states were invited to observe the armistice in Korea; in 1955 Austria was released from occupation into the state of 'neutrality for ever', and in 1957 and 1962 Cambodia and Laos respectively also became internationally regionalised (developments in Asia have, however, eroded this concept; the Vietnam war made neutralism obsolete in Cambodia after 1970 with terrible consequences). The stagnation of political integration in Western Europe, the neutralist option adopted by most newly independent states in the Third World as well as recent detente politics may all have added to the growing interest in neutralism.

PREMISES OF THE NEUTRALISM CONCEPT
Recent ideas about neutralism rarely envisage absolute neutrality of the classic kind. After opting for neutralism, no modern European country would become a 'neutrum'. With respect to social order, such countries would still belong to the West or the East. It is perhaps reasonable to envisage 'differential, relative or qualified neutrality' (Riklin). The term 'neutral corner' used in boxing is appropriate: the European powers can opt for corners not occupied by the superpowers, in an effort 'to abstain from the confrontation between the two big powers', as the Finnish formula reads. The neutralism of Third World non-aligned countries offers another analogy for European neutralism. Neutralism is there regarded as 'a special case of non-alignment with respect to the East-West conflict and the Cold War related to it. In contrast to the neutrals the neutralists do not consider themselves tied to the classic law of neutrality. In the event of war they consider any option to be open to them'.[13]

In two important respects the current debates in the West German peace movement differ from the neutralism debate of the fifties. The first is that neutralism should not serve as an instrument for reunification. Peace in Europe nowadays is valued as a higher objective than German reunification. Secondly, neutralism is not considered as a broad concept in developing 'a third way' between East and West, a new European identity. The neutralism concept of today is discussed in the narrowest possible manner, as an option predominantly for security and alliance politics.

Within the range of alternative options to current defence policies, the neutralist posture is one of the less radical proposals (when compared with a reorientation to purely defensive strategies, the proposals for defence based on low-level violence, or with respect to general and complete disarmament).

MAIN ELEMENTS OF CURRENT NEUTRALISM

The concept consists of two main elements: in Europe there would be a special zone which is free of nuclear arms, and this zone would opt for a neutralist posture in its external relations. Before evaluating these two elements, a definition of the term 'neutralism' is needed. Historically, the term 'neutralism' has had differing meanings.

(1) In international law, which still dominates this debate, neutrality generally means 'non-participation of a state in a war among other states'.[14] Fiedler maintains that 'the element "war" in the beginning was mandatory for neutrality'.[15] The starting point today is the effort to dissociate from the great power rivalries in peacetime, and the strategy is more ambitious than just avoidance of involvement in war.

(2) Efforts by non-aligned countries to abstain from close ties with the blocs have been labelled in the past as 'positive neutralism'; this has usually had negative undertones in both East and West.[16] Nehru's opinion that a neutral position outside the blocs should be positively valued was attacked both by J.F. Dulles *and* Soviet analysts. Subsequently, the value of 'positive neutralism' has been eroded, presumably partly

because of the absolute standards by which the concept was judged.

(3) The changing fate of 'socialist neutrality' has also tarnished the reputation of the neutralist posture.[17] The term was originally used by the Soviet law expert Korovin in 1924, in order to describe the status of the states which formed a *cordon sanitaire* around the then weak Soviet state. Principally, however, in the Soviet perspective 'international relations remain class relations, which by their nature cannot express the indifferent character which is required by neutrality'.[18] Hence a phase of non-aggression and neutrality-treaties in Soviet politics (1923-1933, with Turkey, Germany, Afghanistan, Persia, Finland. . .) was superseded by a phase which contained the concept of 'collective security' (1933-1938); this in turn was followed by a phase of 'socialist neutrality politics'; and after that, the USSR then broke the neutrality of Iran (1941) and Bulgaria (1944). In the early fifties, the USSR heavily criticised the neutrality of Switzerland and Sweden, and maintained that neutrality remains 'an unadmissable means for safe-guarding peace, because it hinders the implementation of the socialist law of development'.[19]

(4) In the heyday of the East-West confrontation, the 'Cold War' between state socialist and capitalist countries, neutrality was viewed as a way of circumventing a clearcut position, just as historically 'in the light of the medieval idea of the *Reich* and the doctrine of just war. . . there was no room for neutralism' (A. Riklin). The decline of the *sacrum imperium* and the emergence of sovereign states was needed to make neutrality possible. In the view of alliance leaders in East and West, the neutralism option still has a certain *defeatist* ring about it—how can one possibly be neutralist in the fierce struggle of ideologies? Neutralist positions in post-war Eastern Europe have been suppressed by the USSR, and in Western Europe traditional neutralist powers like Belgium, the Netherlands and Luxemburg, profoundly affected by the German violation of their neutrality, accepted membership in the Atlantic Alliance.

156

ARGUMENTS AGAINST NEUTRALISM

The main argument against a European neutralist posture is that this would be little more than an intermediate step before the USSR takes control of the rest of the continent. Former Italian defence minister Taviani expressed this fear in an orthodox way: 'there is just one step from denuclearisation to neutrality, and the step from neutralisation to Sovietisation would be even shorter'.[20] It is true that the USSR has for long advocated a neutralist policy for its capitalist neighbour states. There is nothing sinister about this, nothing which is particularly communist about it. Rather it is the rational stance of a power which is making every effort to disengage from a direct confrontation with its antagonist.

A second version of this argument is known as 'Finlandisation'. Based on an analogy with Finnish politics (one which hardly any Finn would accept), Finlandisation implies that a neutral zone in Europe might be unduly influenced by the USSR, and that the fear of diplomatic blackmail might degrade foreign policy positions.

Even if we were, for the sake of argument, to accept that Finnish foreign policies are 'Finlandised' it is questionable whether the term is appropriate for Central Europe. West Germany and other states in the region are not in the same position as Finland—they have never been part of the Russian empire (as Finland was): they represent a much larger economic and political potential, which is much harder to penetrate than Finland, and they are not situated at the periphery of Europe where other powers have little interest. The argument about 'Finlandisation' can be turned upside down; in fact, neutralism offers a greater freedom of action for Europe than membership in the alliances, this freedom is in the interest of the Soviet Union, and this is well understood by the Soviet leadership.

Conservative commentators also tend to have an ambiguous view of 'Finlandisation'. Pierre Hassner advocates a more open, more elastic understanding of security, when he maintains: 'As long as NATO and the Warsaw Pact persist, Finlandisation is the worst Western Europe has to be afraid of, but also the best Eastern Europe can hope for'.[21] In the end, neutralism is certainly linked with certain risks, not the least those tied to the policies and strategies of the USSR. The continuation of present postures also carries formidable risks; the European powers are thus confronted with the choice of differing risks, as far as their security is concerned. In the age of war fighting options, with nuclear weapons limited to the European theatre of war, it appears that the scales are weighted in favour of neutralism rather than continued alliance membership.

FUNCTIONS OF THE NEUTRALIST OPTION

The most important function of neutralism (which in fact first aroused interest in this option) is the contribution it could play in international conflict resolution. This is something in the history of neutralism. In the state of non-war between the two big powers, their relations remain characterised by the arms race, and the excessive accumulation of means of mass destruction. In both economic and ideological spheres, the pattern of conflict resolution in this state of non-war is shaped by such patterns of accumulation. Both sides try to gain the support of third parties not so much for military reasons (in the nuclear age, conventionally armed small and medium states are alliance partners of doubtful value), but rather in pursuit of a claimed legitimacy. By rejecting participation in the East-West ideological dispute and opting for neutralism, it might be possible, at least, to mute this heated struggle.

Neutralism could also influence the methods of warfare. Traditionally, small and medium sized states formed alliances in order to improve their military potential so as to deter or to win a war. The neutralist option was preferred only when this promised a greater gain in the game of power.

In the nuclear age, this remained for a while an important reason for forming an alliance. Some of the lesser powers, afraid of atomic weapons and aware of the impossibility of independent nuclear forces, sought alliance with one of the two great powers.

Today this incentive for partnership with a major nuclear power seems to have been reversed. The sophistication of nuclear means of mass destruction, the overkill capacities on both sides, and the emerging first-strike capabilities all

158

undermine the belief that the alliance leader really is committed to the use of atomic weapons if one or other of the smaller partners face an emergency. The decision to use nuclear weapons will be based, today much more than yesterday, solely on the national interest of the state providing these weapons, i.e. one of the great powers. The neutralism option hence gains in attraction: it offers a clearcut option instead of a nuclear guarantee with doubtful validity.

The major political function of the neutralist option would depend on the ways in which neutralism might influence the dynamics of European politics. It is usually argued that the political stability of Europe would vanish if there is 'decoupling' from American strategies. The recent debate about defence postures has, however, strongly implied that the security interests of the US (and the USSR) in some instances differ or even contradict the security requirements of smaller European powers. Moreover, it is suggested that the alliances would not weaken symmetrically: the West would lose much more in alliance cohesion, given the fact that the US is not a European power, and that the Eastern bloc is much more tightly organised because of the nature of the political systems in Eastern Europe and the Soviet Union.

While one could conceive of the disengagement of Western Europe to some extent, from US tutelage, sceptics ask whether anything similar could take place in Eastern Europe. Surprisingly enough, the Soviet leadership has repeatedly indicated its readiness to talk in more political terms about relations in Central Europe than is usually assumed. The proof is provided by several statements in the course of past detente politics, which have been mostly overlooked, because the arms control content of these messages appeared to be more relevant for the success of detente strategies. For example, in May 1966, the USSR indicated in a note willingness to negotiate a reduction of troops in East Germany and West Germany (opening up the possibility of a zone of reduced armaments). The well-known 'Bucharest declaration' of July 1966 contains, *inter alia,* an offer to talk about a nuclear-free zone, and a repetition of the May proposal about arms reductions in the two German states. At the Karlsbad

Conference of April 1967 Soviet leaders addressed the possibilities for reducing tension between East and West by withdrawing foreign troops from German soil. The Western response, the consent to negotiate troop reductions in Europe (ending in the Vienna MBFR negotiations), can also be regarded as a bridge in the direction of the disengagement idea: massive troop reductions, which could lead to a militarily thinned-out zone in the area under negotiation could be regarded as an intermediate step towards much more radical political solutions than are ever debated in Western elite circles. Progress towards mutual force reductions in Europe, despite the recent impasse, also offers dynamic possibilities of a *relance Européene;* hence, the argument about disengagement or neutralism is much less hypothetical than is usually assumed.

The 'neutralist option' is a combination of gradual measures rather than a fixed, inflexible posture. It is not the classic, well known concept of *absolute neutrality,* but rather a graduated, much more flexible process of *neutralism,* which does not require a radical reorientation of the states concerned. Underlying the argument is the notion that peace in Europe would be much more stable than under the threat of mutual assured destruction if the conventional play of political forces, the recognition of differing security interests, is no longer suppressed. This is not a plea for old-fashioned nationalism in military politics—on the contrary, the neutralist as well as the nuclear-free option can be adopted by a cluster of European states, which would act collectively. The renunciation of nationalism has been an important achievement in past European politics, and the security interests of all states concerned will be much better served if their governments opt collectively and coordinate their policies jointly in the direction of disengagement rather than confrontation.

NOTES

1. Cf. George F. Kennan, *Russia, the Atom and the West,* the book version of his famed *Reith lectures* in the BBC in 1957. The third and fourth lecture are the ones dealing with our topic. Cf. for a general evaluation also: Eugene Hinterhoff, *Disengagement,* London 1959, esp. p. 217.
2. The Eden Plan can be found in his opening address to the Geneva summit at July 18, 1955 (cf. e.g. *Europa-Archiv,* 16/1955, p. 8104, or Eden's

Memoirs, pp. 339). Cf. also Hinterhoff, op. cit., p. 97 and 168.

3. Hugh Gaitskell, 'Disengagement: Why? How?', in *Foreign Affairs*, vol. 36, July 1958, p. 551.

4. Quoted (and translated) from Konrad Adenauer, *Erinnerungen 1955-1959*, Stuttgart 1967, p. 147.

5. Quoted from Charles R. Planck, *Sicherheit in Europa. Die Vorschläge für Rüstungsbeschränkung und Abrüstung 1955 bis 1965*, Munich 1968, p. 114.

6. The details of these developments, and other arms reduction proposals, can be taken from: Hans-Gert Pöttering, *Adenauers Sicherheitspolitik 1955-63*, Dusseldorf 1975, pp. 140. Rapacki's original speech was delivered to the 12th General Assembly of the UN at October 2, 1957 (Cf. *Europa-Archiv*, 2/1958, pp. 10 482).

7. The best account is provided by Rainer Dohse, *Der Dritte Weg. Neutralitätsbestrebungen in Westdeutschland zwischen 1945 und 1955*, Hamburg, 1974.

8. At the founding meeting in London in April 1980, where I was present, most speakers stressed that Britain did not have an 'appeal culture', and that hence the prospects of this initiative were highly doubtful. The breakthrough at the Labour Party Conference and other events can be easily studied in the periodical, *European Nuclear Disarmament Bulletin.*

9. Mary Kaldor, 'Why we need European Nuclear Disarmament' in *ADIU Report* (Armament & Disarmament Information Unit, Brighton), vol. 3, no. 1, January/February 1981.

10. Cf. handbook articles like Heinz Fiedler 'Neutralität' in: C.D. Kernig (ed.), *Marxismus im Systemvergleich* (Marxism in the comparison of systems), New York and Frankfurt, series politics, vol. 3, 1973; or Alois Riklin, 'Neutralität', in: Wichard Wyoke (ed.), *Handwörterbuch internationale Politik*, Opladen 1977.

11. Cf. Fiedler, op. cit., p. 263.

12. 'West German Poll finds 43% back neutralist policy', in: *International Herald Tribune*, August 20, 1980, p. 2.

13. Riklin, op. cit., p. 240.

14. Ibid., p. 241.

15. Fiedler, op. cit., p. 258.

16. Cf. Fritz Schatten (F.S.), Positiver Neutralismus, in: Carola Stern/Thilo Vogelsang/Erhard Klöss/Albert Graff (eds.), *dtv-Lexikon zur Geschichte und Politik im 20. Jahrhundert*, vol. 3, Munich 1973, p. 651.

17. Cf. Fiedler, op. cit., p. 259.

18. Ibid.

19. Ibid., p. 267.

20. Quoted from 'Hubertus Prinz zu Löwenstein and Volkmar von Zühlsdorff, *Die Verteidigung des Westens*, Bonn 1960, p. 333.

21. Pierre Hassner, 'Schwankendes Europa' in: Raina, Peter (ed.), *Internationale Politik in den siebziger Jahren*, Frankfurt/M, 1973, pp. 72-87.

ALTERNATIVE DEFENCE POLICIES AND MODERN WEAPON TECHNOLOGY

Ben Dankbaar

Within the peace movement and among peace researchers there is growing interest in alternative defence strategies. The increasing political importance of the peace movement makes it necessary for us to think about alternatives to the defence system we are opposing. This is not a simple thing to do. People disagree on whether alternatives are really necessary. It is argued that many of the fears and feelings of animosity which justify the present defence system originate from that same system. Therefore if the system disappears, the fears and aggressions will disappear with it leaving no need for an alternative defence system. This extreme position in favour of complete and unilateral disarmament is not shared by everyone in the peace movement. Many activists recognise a need for security which in the present system of nation states has been partially satisfied by military defence systems. Their criticism of the existing defence system is that it contributes less and less to security, creates instabilities and uses up ever more scarce resources that are needed for other purposes. This criticism is directed against nuclear weapons which now have less and less to do with the stability of mutual deterrence and a nuclear war limited to Europe seems more likely than ever.

Concern about the possibility of a nuclear war in Europe is not confined to the peace movement. There are military people who are worried about it too. They see that they would have failed if the military defence of Europe were to lead to its destruction. So, naturally, they plead for a stronger conventional defence of Western Europe. But 'more of the same' is of no interest to the peace movement. Not only would such defence use up even more resources, but as things stand, it would also lead to incredible destruction. However, in recent years some military writers have proposed ideas on alternative defence systems that would entail important structural changes in the defence system. A number of these ideas have also influenced thinking about alternatives within the peace movement.

Alternative defence policies emphasise the need for a purely defensive strategy. Only a purely defensive posture, which does not threaten the opponent but does satisfy a justified need for security, can be a credible starting point for a process of disarmament.[1] The interesting thing about the new military alternatives is that they too emphasise a defensive posture. They introduce modern weapon technologies which are claimed to be defensive.

Under the influence of military writers, thinking about alternative defence strategies in the peace movement has become much more concrete and militarised. Military methods now at times seem acceptable as part of an alternative defence strategy. The detail and military content of these alternatives revive long-standing differences over their nature and status. Whilst some people think that a real alternative defence strategy must be associated with far-ranging social change, others see it more as a functional substitute: the existing defence system is replaced by a better one without necessitating further changes in the rest of society. The recent military alternatives seem to support the latter point of view. They are presented as optimal solutions to the security problems of existing governments. If we take a closer look, all this turns out not to be so simple. The existing defence system is also presented as the optimal solution to the security problems of governments. In addition, the existing defence system is firmly anchored in a whole complex of institutional relationships, economic interests and personal convictions.

One of the cornerstones of this complex is the conviction that the West must base its defence on technological superiority. This conviction has governed defence thinking in the United States and the rest of the western world. Its origins can be found in the success of the Manhattan Project that delivered the atomic bomb in the Second World War.

Combined with the industrial capacities of the West, this belief in high technology has created enormously complex weapon-systems incorporating countless functions in one big machine, interrelated by electronic communications systems, flying radar systems, satellites, etc. In fact, it has brought us the permanent technological arms race, with all its destabilising elements, and a permanent threat to any kind of disarmament treaty. Alternative defence strategies traditionally emphasise the role of people instead of machines. Significantly, the new military alternatives are also very critical of the complex weapon system; the military-industrial complex that created these systems is criticised from within. This aspect of alternative military strategies shows that if they are to contribute to a different, more peaceful world then in the end they will probably be associated with far-reaching social changes.

ALTERNATIVE DEFENCE STRATEGIES IN HISTORY

Thinking about alternative defence systems already has a long tradition in the socialist and labour movements. In fact, this tradition goes back even further, to the bourgeois critique of the professional standing armies of the 18th century. Instead of the professional armies, full of criminals and adventurers, that were used by European royalty to fight each other, the bourgeoisie proposed the democratic ideal of the 'nation in arms'. Armies should not serve the interests of a corrupt elite, but the interests of the nation. The Napoleonic wars and the introduction of several variants of conscription in almost all European states during the 19th century showed that a 'nation in arms' is not only useful for democratic or exclusively defensive purposes. Marx and Engels, the great theoreticians of the labour movement, held on to the ideal of arming the people, but they emphasised that the people, i.e. the working class, would have to be in charge. During the last quarter of the 19th century social-democratic parties campaigned for the introduction of general conscription, coupled with a dissolution of the standing armies, substituting for them a militia system. The least they asked for was a decided shortening of the period conscripts had to stay in the army, to prevent them becoming indoctrinated. The

165

leader of the French socialists, Jean Jaurès, developed these ideas further in his book on the New Army (*L'Armeé Nouvelle,* 1911). He was also clearly inspired by the Swiss militia-system, the system which inspired those who criticised the standing armies of the 18th century. In a militia-system, the armed forces consist almost entirely of civilians, who are called up to serve in times of danger.

In the 1920s and '30s these alternative concepts gave way to pacifist currents that opposed any use of armed force. In the Soviet Union, the proponents of militia-type forces and partisan warfare did not get the chance to put their ideas into practice in the development of the Red Army. After the Second World War pacifist tendencies were again important, especially in the struggle against nuclear weapons. Some of the older ideas on alternative defence strategies, however, surfaced again in the concept of civilian, non-violent defence. In his influential book *Defence in the Nuclear Age,* 1958, Stephen King-Hall advocated civilian defence as a viable alternative to the nuclear threat. The absolute violence of the atomic bomb was opposed by the absolute non-violence of civilian defence. Since then, many theoretical and historical studies have been published on this subject, ranging from the activities of Gandhi in India to the Czech resistance against the Soviet invasion in 1968.[2] Typical of this approach is the defence of cultural and other values, rather than of national territory. The proposed techniques are those of non-cooperation, strikes, demonstrations, an appeal to the moral values of the opponent and sometimes sabotage. Civilian defence is non-violent and engages almost the total population. It therefore depends to a large extent on the morale and self-confidence of the people, who will have to deal with possible violent reprisals by the enemy.

In the course of time many objections have been made to the concept of civilian defence.[3] Civilian defence is said to have insufficient historical precedents; it probably cannot face up to extreme repression; it cannot defend outlying and thinly-populated areas; it is not an effective deterrent to prevent foreign attack in the first place; and it requires an improbably homogeneous, disciplined and nationalistic population. The theory and practice of civilian defence have not been able to do away with all these objections, at least not to everybody's satisfaction. Some people therefore suggest that it cannot be considered a good alternative everywhere and always, and that it should be 'mixed' with other forms of 'violent' military and non-military defence. Others oppose the idea of a mix between military and civilian defence methods, claiming that non-violence is the essence of a civilian defence strategy, which would be made ineffective by association with violent means of resistance.

The more pragmatic approach drops absolute non-violence, but still opposes weapons of mass destruction. Alternative strategies with military components then become acceptable, if escalation to the level of mass destruction is excluded and if the destruction caused by this strategy remains limited and controllable. Also the idea that control over territory is unimportant has been qualified. Values and territory are not as easy to separate as the theory of civilian defence sometimes assumed.

An important source of inspiration for the peace movement as well as the military advocates of alternative defence strategies has been the war in Vietnam. The victory of small, technologically inferior Vietnam called everywhere for a reappraisal of political components of warfare, the value of morale and the relative significance of advanced technology. The works on guerrilla warfare by Mao and Giap were studied all over the world, not only by revolutionaries, but also by officers in military academies throughout the West. In Europe, apart from Switzerland, Yugoslavia attracted attention, as its defence system is partly based on its experience of partisan warfare during the Second World War.

TERRITORIAL DEFENCE
All these influences can be found in Adam Roberts' book on *Territorial Defence,* 1976. The book exemplifies a·new way of thinking about alternative defence strategies, using more military elements than before. Among other things it describes the defence systems of Sweden and Yugoslavia. Important differences from the strategy of civilian defence are the use of violence, the important role of regular armed forces (albeit of a militia type) and the central organising role of the state.

Much becomes clear in Roberts' definition of territorial defence:

> Territorial defence is a system of defence in depth: it is the governmentally-organised defence of a state's own territory, conducted on its own territory. It is aimed at creating a situation in which an invader, even though he may at least for a time gain geographical possession of part or all of the territory, is constantly harassed and attacked from all sides. It is a form of defence strategy which has important organisational implications, being liable to involve substantial reliance on a citizen army, including local units of a militia type. Characteristically, a territorial defence system is based on weapons systems, strategies and methods of military organisation which are better suited to their defensive role than to engagement in major military actions abroad.[4]

Roberts describes Sweden and Yugoslavia, because they both have a system of territorial defence which combines militia-type units with regular units whose task is to gain time for mobilising and organising the militia. As such, these countries might have more ideas to offer on alternative defence strategies for Western Europe than the pure militia-system of Switzerland. At the same time, Roberts points out the limits of territorial defence. As with civilian defence, territorial defence has no definitive answer to nuclear attack. Every urban society is extremely vulnerable to nuclear or even conventional bombing and territorial defence, which renounces the means to attack an enemy likewise, can only provide limited protection. A well-organised territorial defence can only be used to show the enemy that nothing can be gained from such bombing. If the cities are bombed, the defence system will still remain intact. The enemy is offered the choice between a senseless and immoral act of destruction or a very costly effort to occupy the country. Occupation will also be very costly to the defenders. Even if the enemy does not engage in bombing or other acts of reprisal, territorial defence might by its extensive use of territory and time, lead to large-scale destruction. Roberts emphasises that a well-prepared territorial defence is not only, and not in the first place, a potential alternative for the existing defence system; it also has an important deterrent value.

Lastly, there is also the problem of how territorial defence can end a conflict. Should one just hope that the enemy will retreat exasperated and frustrated by the omnipresent resistance? How long does the system of territorial defence hold out before it falls apart? Should the aim be to get the enemy to the negotiating table? There are some examples of territorial defence leading straight to negotiation and a peace settlement. Most writers, however, emphasise the need to wage a more formal battle on a higher level of violence towards the end of the conflict. In that case heavier military units with more offensive equipment would be needed. If these are not included in the original defence set-up, the country will have to depend on outside support. The writings on guerrilla warfare by Mao and Giap insist on the importance of regular armed forces in the last phase of the conflict. Of course, in the actual historical experience of China and Vietnam, these forces were heavily dependent on outside support.

The concepts of civilian and territorial defence largely continue the alternative defence concepts of the 19th century social democrats. The purely defensive orientation and the involvement of the whole population are typical of all of the concepts. Twentieth century variants also emphasise the level of violence. This is not surprising in view of the unheard-of possibilities for destruction that the advance of technology has created in this century. It is surprising though, that in the debates on alternative defence policies very little was said for a long time about developments in military technology. This did not seem necessary in the discussion of civilian defence which rejected any use of (military) violence, but of course military technology, and most of all the nuclear threat, naturally played an important role as a backdrop to the argument. Discussions in the peace movement about territorial and guerrilla defence very often drew a romantic picture of those struggles; machine-guns were the most advanced weapons people talked about. In fact most of the discussions dealt with situations in remote Third World countries. These alternative concepts were not used to appraise the defence policies of NATO countries. Of course the prospects for such an appraisal were not very promising.

It was obvious that modern military technology was pushing the armed forces further and further away from the idea of a nation in arms. Instead, manpower in the armed forces was replaced by increasingly complex weapons systems, the armed forces were turning into one giant automatic fighting machine and some generals were dreaming aloud of an automated battlefield. In the last decade, increasing doubts about the effectiveness of complex weapons systems in relation to their enormous costs have cooled some of this enthusiasm. New developments in arms technology also seem to point in a different direction. The concept of territorial defence has been resurrected by several military writers in connection with the introduction of highly advanced military equipment.[5]

TECHNO-COMMANDOS

Although his work is best known for the concept of territorial defence he spells out, Horst Afheldt also deals extensively with nuclear strategy.[6] In fact Afheldt places himself in the tradition of the 'arms control' school of the late 1950s. The work of this school was centred on the stability of the nuclear strategic balance. Afheldt builds on the concept of stable deterrence developed at that time. Stable deterrence means that both sides possess invulnerable nuclear arms, with which they can inflict unacceptable damage on the opponent. Using this concept, he criticises the development of American strategic doctrine in the '70s because it shows a tendency to search for military advantages at the strategic level. On the other hand, he accepts the possibility of making nuclear strikes which cause only limited, acceptable damage, as part of his alternative defence strategy for West Germany. Afheldt assumes that in the future the Unites States will continue to take a great interest in the existence of West Germany as an independent nation. In the event of war then, the Americans can be called upon to force the Soviet Union into retreat. East European governments could be forced by a nuclear threat to limit drastically their support for Soviet military operations. The idea is not to attack the Soviet Union directly in a way that would destabilise the strategic balance between the superpowers, but to threaten the leaders of the Soviet

Union with the loss of their control over Eastern Europe, which Afheldt argues is so important to them that they would come to their senses. These nuclear strikes would have to be carried out from submarines. Afheldt emphasises that the nuclear strikes should serve purely political purposes and not military ones. If threats were not enough the strikes would have to be directed against the economic infra-structure of Eastern Europe.

One may well wonder whether the opponent will experience the difference between military and political nuclear strikes just as clearly. Nor is it clear why such strikes would not call forth retaliation against German cities. Anyway most people in the peace movement reject any nuclear means in an alternative defence strategy because of the danger of escalation and level of destruction involved. For Afheldt, nuclear means solve the problem we noticed earlier. The system of territorial defence he proposes can slow down an opponent (and therefore prevent a *fait accompli,* which might make the American nuclear threat less convincing) and raise the costs of aggression for the enemy, but it lacks the means to force the enemy into retreat, since all offensive weapons systems have been abandoned (see below). Still it is possible to take the conventional elements out of Afheldt's concept and see them as an alternative defence strategy. In that case one would have to rely on the high deterrence value of the territorial defence system, or, in the event of war, hope that a successful territorial defence will eventually bring the enemy to the negotiating table and to retreat.

The territorial defence strategy that Afheldt developed for West Germany is based on a set of norms. The most important of these are: the enemy should not be offered military targets worth attacking with heavy means of destruction (i.e. nuclear missiles); the level of violence must remain limited and fully under control; there is no need for West Germany to possess a capacity for military interventions around the world.

Such reasoning results in a defence strategy without aircraft, airports, tanks, heavy infantry vehicles and large missile systems, all of which would be worthwhile targets for the enemy. The present NATO strategy of forward

171

defence shows an abundance of militarily important targets
on both sides. Attacks on these targets would bring about
the destruction of West Germany. The focussing of defence
at the border leads to a strong concentration of troops,
again offering the enemy worthwhile targets for heavy means
of destruction. Contrary to this, Afheldt proposes to cover
the entire territory of West Germany with a network of
'techno-commandos'. These are units of 15 to 20 soldiers,
divided into about five groups. The units will be armed with
anti-tank guided missiles (Afheldt mentions the short-range,
wire-guided Milan, that can be operated by two men) and a
few longer-range (at least 25 kilometres) guided missiles.
Each unit must defend an area of about 20 square kilometres. In peacetime the unit is permanently stationed in
that area, exercises there and prepares defensive positions
and hide-outs. If it comes to war, the unit uses its knowledge of the terrain and its prepared positions to destroy
as many tanks as possible. After they have used up their
weapons supply, they are free to retreat, spread out or
hide. The network of techno-commandos has the task of
'absorbing' the tank forces of the Warsaw Pact in an endless
series of small fights while they advance towards the Rhine.
Cities will not be part of the network so that they will not
become theatres of fighting. The network does not offer any
targets for massive destruction: there are no concentrations
of troops, no heavy units, no airforce and no logistic
apparatus.

Afheldt expects that such a network of autonomous
techno-commandos can at least prevent the much feared
fait accompli of an occupation of West Germany in a few
days. As such, it can also be considered a trustworthy non-
nuclear deterrent.

During the fighting period, which will end only after all of
West Germany is occupied, there will be ample time for
political decision making. This will involve threatening and
pressurising Eastern Europe without being forced by military
exigencies into unwelcome political moves.

Since the techno-commandos are static forces, confined to
their limited area they cannot be used in an aggressive or
escalatory way. They come into action only after their area

has been attacked. This might bring the enemy to attack over a very narrow front, cutting the country into smaller segments. To prevent this, the units have longer-range missiles, to make an attack over a front of less than 50 kilometres unattractive. Of course these missiles should not be so large and complex that they might form meaningful targets for destruction. Afheldt suggests here the use of mini cruise missiles. To prevent air-borne attacks, the network of local autonomous techno-commandos would have to be supplemented by light, mobile techno-commandos, possibly of a militia-type, to be called up and organised by the static units. In addition small groups of light surface-to-air missiles should be stationed all over the territory of West Germany. Perhaps there should even be one group for every techno-commando area. Peacetime strength for a force like this, covering all of West Germany is estimated to be about 350–400,000. This number should be compared to the 775,000 troops (excluding the air force and naval forces, 1974), now present on the territory of the West Germany and the Benelux states.

Afheldt took the idea of autonomous units from the work of the French major Guy Brossolet (see below). The designation techno-commandos was introduced by Afheldt to signify that these units use advanced, so-called precision-guided munitions (PGM). According to Afheldt the present trends in weapons technology are favourable for the kind of territorial defence he proposes. The introduction of micro-electronics and sensor technology makes it possible with relatively cheap missiles to trace, hit and destroy expensive complex weapons systems like tanks and airplanes with a very high degree of efficiency (one shot, one kill). If technology is already providing these missiles, it must be possible to direct innovation and produce even better weapons suitable for territorial defence.

A lot has been written about the implications of these precision-guided munitions for the strategy and tactics of NATO. A flood of publications has appeared on the subject since the 1973 war in the Middle East in which the weapons were enormously effective against tanks and airplanes.[7] There is almost general agreement that PGMs have improved the possibilities for defence. Whether this really means the end of the domination of the tank and airplane on the battlefield remains a hotly debated issue. This is not surprising since all post Second World War armed forces have been built around such weapons systems which have been enlarged and improved many times. The idea that they would now be threatened by a relatively simple kind of weapon, operated by one or two infantry soldiers, means a revolution in the image of war that undermines established positions of power in the armed forces as well as in the arms industry.

MILITARY WRITERS

The proposals for a territorial defence of West Germany by Horst Afheldt should be considered as part of a much wider series of proposals and suggestions by several military and non-military writers.[8] Some go for radical changes in strategy, others speak in terms of adding to and improving on the existing NATO strategy. In West Germany all these ideas have attracted quite a bit of attention, which is understandable since giving up the forward defence strategy is traditionally equated with handing over the country for destruction. Simultaneously with Afheldt's book two other studies were published in West Germany, one by the Austrian General Emil Spannocchi and the other by the French Major Guy Brossolet. Whereas the ideas of the Frenchman do not seem to have much influence in his own country (Brossolet was promoted to a post in the embassy in Peking), General Spannocchi is trying to implement his ideas as commander of the Austrian Army.

Spannocchi's central problem is the defence of a small and neutral state in Central Europe. He points out that Austria does not have an answer to a nuclear attack. It is a fact that must be accepted because nothing can be done about it. However, it remains absolutely necessary to build a defence system which makes it impossible for NATO or the Warsaw Pact to walk over Austria in either direction. Only then is Austria's proclaimed neutrality really credible. Spannocchi, of course, does not want to deny that both power blocs can win a war against Austria. He wants to prevent Austria becoming part of the theatre of war in an East-West conflict.

Therefore an invasion of Austria must be made as difficult and as unattractive as possible.

The power of both military blocs lies in their technological superiority, says Spannocchi.

> They use their superiority there, where it is abundantly available: in technology. They became leading powers, because they are super-industrialized countries. And the laws of this super-industrialization form the basis for all their plans.[9]

A large power will use technology against the small power and the one thing a small country should not do is to try to match this technological potential, by duplicating the armed forces of the big powers on a smaller scale. A small country should use the principles of guerrilla warfare instead, as developed by Mao, Giap and others, since they demonstrate a method of fighting by the weak against the strong. Accordingly, Spannocchi develops guidelines for the defence of Austria: there will not be one big battle, but a very large number of small ones. Each of these actions will necessarily be lost, but they will cost the enemy dearly. There shall be no movement in large units. The enemy should be allowed to take over some of the classical points of defence, but should not be allowed a real military victory. The enemy must be forced to use more infantry instead of the heavy, complex weapons systems in which his advantage lies. The final goal is to force the enemy to fill up the whole counntry with infantry, which would be an unacceptable cost to a superpower.

On the basis of these guidelines, Spannocchi proposes a mixed system, consisting of a mobile, professional standing army and a large system of militia units. The militia units should be seen as the most important part of the system whilst the professional army is charged with limited border defence and gaining time for the militia units to be mobilised and deployed. Even partisans (armed citizens without official military status) would take part in the defence system, mainly for communication purposes. Spannocchi strongly emphasises the importance of a good system of leadership and control. Guerrilla warfare may seem to be a chaotic

175

affair, but it is not without reason that Mao and Giap stress the decisive role of the party.

> Giap points out time and again the decisive role of the party. To the extent that he is speaking of the functions of a system of leadership, he is completely correct; but communism doesn't have to be a precondition for that.[10]

This means it is necessary for Austria to develop a political and administrative system that can function as did the communist party in China and Vietnam, creating political and ideological coherence in the country. There will also have to be a regional military command system because it is thought the struggle will be widely spread out. Modern electronics would have to play an important role in the communications network between fighting units and higher levels of command.

Guy Brossolet provided Afheldt with his concept of techno-commandos. Brossolet is highly critical of the idea that the defence of France must take the form of a classical battle. He has two major arguments for this position. First, he argues that the meaning and significance of the battle has changed ever since the arrival of the atomic bomb. Since it is not on the battlefield that the most decisive weapons are deployed, the battle is not fought in order to 'win'. The battle is fought to show readiness to defend oneself and to demonstrate the political will to use nuclear weapons if necessary. A classical tank battle, however, is not the only way to serve these purposes. Second, Brossolet raises serious doubts about whether the present armed forces can conduct a real battle. The growing complexity of the armed forces has created serious probelms in logistics, communications and the motivation of soldiers. Field exercises reveal that these problems make the outcome of a battle in effect a matter of chance.

Brossolet proposes to break down the present hierarchical system of the forces which are preparing for a large-scale tank battle and to set up independently operating units, each armed and motivated to defend their own piece of territory. About 2500 of these light 'modules' of 15 to 20 soldiers would have to fill up an area of 60,000 square kilometres, stretching from the Channel to Switzerland. Each light module must fight all enemy units, especially tanks and other armoured formations, which enter their designated area of about 20 square kilometres. This deployment of forces will result in a 'non-battle'; there will be a long series of small fights with a statistically predictable outcome which is not a matter of chance. Differing from Afheldt, Brossolet also wants to deploy about 200 heavy modules, with three anti-tank helicopters each, and a number of tank-modules with 54 tanks each, to carry out counter attacks and to defend open areas. Brossolet calculates that about 80,000 soldiers including support units, would be needed for this system of territorial defence. Again, it should be pointed out that PGMs play an important role in the strategy which is why Brossolet uses the term 'scientific guerrillas'. Spannocchi and Brossolet's alternative policies (like Afheldt's) are meant to gain time for negotiations and decisions about, for example, in the case of France the eventual use of nuclear weapons, and in the case of Austria the intervention of the allies. Strategic nuclear deterrence is a consistent feature of all these alternatives.

The contributions of two other German authors show how varied and widespread the debate on territorial defence is: Major-General A.D. Jochen Löser and General Franz Uhle-Wettler. Both argue for more infantry and some measure of territorial defence for West Germany. Their publications have provoked extensive debate. As expected, their views have been rejected by the West German Ministry of Defence.[11]

Löser criticises the strategy of flexible response and particularly forward defence on the grounds that the present relation of forces makes it impracticable and it could lead to the destruction of Germany. A huge increase in the military budget and build-up of all parts of the allied conventional forces might be one way out. But this seems very unlikely and anyway does not tackle what is wrong with the forces structure. Too much reliance on complex weapons systems has left too few troops to have a real forward defence:

177

The high mechanization and the arms programmes that have been decided upon often more for political than for military reasons, have their price. AWACS and Tornado are just two examples. Mechanization calls for ever more logistics, the new systems require corresponding munitions. The proportion of combat troops to support and logistics is in the Federal Republic of Germany already down to 30:70. In other NATO countries the proportion is even worse.[12]

Löser therefore proposes to restructure the forces by increasing the infantry, giving them anti-tank weapons and deploying them in depth. Infantry forces should serve as the shield whilst the existing NATO tank forces would remain the sword. However, the tank forces should not be used up in a large tank battle. Instead they should fight a long series of small battles in close cooperation with the infantry.

Uhle-Wettler, chief of planning at NATO headquarters (SHAPE), also proposes an increase in infantry but reaches this conclusion after a critical analysis of the tactical and operational concepts of the German Bundeswehr. He points out that the border areas of West Germany, where the fighting is supposed to take place, consist mainly of villages and forests. According to official army estimates, in 55 per cent of this area, visibility is less than 500 metres at most. Uhle-Wettler questions what the troops can do with some of their fine equipment which can only be used over distances of more than 500 metres. In fact, tank-brigades and mechanised infantry brigades have become so similar now that neither can operate effectively in difficult terrain. He proposes restricting the heavy brigades to open areas and replacing those in forest and built-up areas with real infantry. These forces should be armed with PGMs and operate in small, widely spread-out groups. They should not be provided with trucks or armoured cars, but use requisitioned tractors and agricultural vehicles to transport their equipment and munitions.[13]

COMPLEXITY AND READINESS

All the alternative defence policies put forward by both military and civilian writers contain some explicit or implicit criticism of modern complex weapons systems. Uhle-Wettler for instance subtitles his book, 'The danger of overtechnization of the armed forces'. He writes:

> Only seldom is it asked, what price we pay for the technization and what disadvantages the advantages bring with them. It seems old-fashioned to ask, if not already in some areas a surplus of techniza-tion is forcing us to develop new, more simple forms. Technology dominates the minds of soldiers too and they let themselves be fascinated by the successes of mechanized divisions in the Second World War and later, although these successes were gained on a very different terrain. If someone points at the price and the possible dangers and limits of technization, his remarks are usually dismissed without further investigation.[14]

That someone is obviously Uhle-Wettler himself, who writes 50 pages about the price of introducing technology, and he includes the following points: in modern armies, there are fewer combatants in every unit; the physical and intellectual quality of these combatants is getting worse; the dependence on new supplies has enormously increased the logistic appara-tus; mobility and firepower are very specialised for specific situations and terrain, which means that they are useless half the time; complex weapons systems require large supplies of spare parts and much servicing to keep them going; because of rising costs, armies are becoming smaller all the time.

Some of these complaints are already quite long standing and will be acknowledged especially in the smaller NATO countries where financial pressure has been felt much earlier. Interestingly, these remarks are now also heard from the Pentagon, although as yet they are not linked with proposals to change the structure of the armed forces. Franklin Spinney points out in a paper (1980) that increasingly complex weapons systems have been bought at the expense of readi-ness. Increasing complexity however is increasing the cost even of low readiness:

> We are currently in a state of low readiness, we have fielded equip-ment that is much more difficult to maintain (when viewed from the entire support base) at a high level of material readiness, and we face unprecedented manpower problems—particularly in the

high skill areas. Although in the past, short-term modernisation growth could be financed out of short-term readiness reductions, this may be much less feasible in the future. Even if low readiness were deemed acceptable for the next five years, the rising costs of low readiness could require either decreases in investment growth or unplanned increases in the overall budget.[15]

Spinney goes on to point out that, in the past, increased budgets led to new investment programmes without adequate provisions for support and maintenance.[16] He then asks if increasing complexity and cost have actually increased capability. Combat experience seem to be ambiguous on this point:

For example, in the case of air-to-air combat, it is not clear that increasing avionics complexity has yielded combat dividends that warrant the cost growth. F-86s using machine guns in Korea got about a 10 to 1 exchange ratio over Korean Mig-15s. In contrast 15 years later, the F-4 in Vietnam, with its complex all-weather beyond visual range (BVR) radar missile capability only achieved about a 2 to 1 exchange ratio against the clear weather, within visual range Mig-21. The lethality of the Sparrow missile, .08 to .13, turned out to be at least a factor of 5 lower than predicted. Many argue that the visual rules of engagement in Vietnam precluded the F-4 from maximizing its BVR capability, and that Vietnam results are not indicative of BVR performance in a European war, because the rules of engagement will be different. Even if this argument were true, and the evidence is not clear on this point, we now find that the benefits of the complex BVR capability are contingent upon precise rules of engagement in an uncertain futute war—namely the authorization to fire at a target before it has been positively identified.[17]

Not only does Spinney attack 'the faith that emerging technology will revolutionize capability and cost', he also points out that the belief in technology leads to a preference for 'quantifiable' characteristics of weapons systems, like lethality, and survivability. Most of these characteristics cannot be measured properly. Moreover the stress on lethality overlooks the fact that capturing enemies is an important element of victory. Surrender often takes place in the face of an overwhelming enemy presence which is more important than lethality. But by deploying fewer and larger systems, presence has been exchanged for lethality. Again we find that the human factor in warfare assumes more importance in the criticism of complex weapons systems. The emphasis is placed on the numbers of infantry soldiers and on the less tangible notion of morale.

CONCLUSION

All the alternative defence proposals criticise modern weapons technology. But this does not mean a general, across-the-board opposition to modern technology. On the contrary these alternatives make use of the most modern types of electronic equipment. What is new about these proposals is that they use modern technology in a way that is unorthodox within the existing defence systems. They emphasise defensive, decentralised operations and decision-making. They have an eye for the morale and motivation of soldiers and involve people in the defence of their homes, instead of 'modernising' them out of the armed forces.

The belief in technology, which has been and still is such an important element in the arms race, has created increasingly complex weapons systems and forces structures. These are exceedingly expensive, more and more ineffective and therefore highly dangerous. Some professional military people recognise the problems and are looking for answers. They suggest simple, but highly effective weapons and a more important role for the human factor. Quite often they are also inspired by ideas about territorial defence and guerrilla warfare. Peace researchers have picked up the same ideas in their attempt to develop the concepts of civilian defence and the 'new democratic army' of Jean Jaurès.

Horst Afheldt, among others, has recognised this confluence of interests in his formulation of an alternative defence policy. Afheldt's strategy not only solves the problems of the military by introducing less complex PGMs, but is also purely defensive. It is designed to create stability and guarantee peace 'with military means'. Afheldt sometimes implies that the advance of weapons technology will automatically force the military to implement his policy. And of course it is true that if the military does not change course the problems analysed by Spinney will become increasingly urgent. This invokes the image of a military concerned to fulfill its obligations and to protect the population in the best way possible. Such a military would cooperate with the electronics industry and kick the older industries out of their established positions within the arms business, in order to realise the alternative aims of the peace movement.[18]

This proposition is of interest to the peace movement and might even be a rational strategy for the military and the electronics industry. But of course it is highly improbable. First, the present defence system has an enormous power base and nothing short of war is likely fundamentally to change it. Structural change in the armed forces might well benefit the electronics industry, but the industry is already doing very well these days in cooperation with the major manufacturers of weapon systems. Second, do governments and the military really see peace as the highest good and most important goal of their policies? Surely the starting point of the peace movement is that the opposite is true and that governments risk war for the sake of other 'vital interests'. Third, the development of military applications in electronics certainly does not always strengthen defensive strategies. One must devise an active policy in order to back up a defensive strategy with modern technology. This has been done in the case of development programmes which are now pushed by all parts of the armed forces.

The peace movement cannot sit back and wait until autonomous changes in military technology enforce the alternative defence strategies of the movement. Introducing alternative defence strategies is not a technical operation but a highly political one. Governments must be forced to take their statements, about peace and stability always coming first, very seriously. This is a task for the peace movement and alternative defence strategies can play an important role. They show a way out of the dilemma of either being armed to the teeth or being defenceless. The important thing about new developments in this field is that they are appropriate for advanced and developed countries. They do not ignore modern technology, but actually use it.

182

Not only does this mean that alternative strategies become more credible, but also the peace movement might find some unexpected allies. Financial strains and 'overtechnisation' have caused some cracks to appear in the massive alliance between industry, the government and the military. By pushing alternative military strategies, the peace movement might be able to divide and weaken its opponents in that complex. It might even receive support from military personnel and from corners of the arms industry. Some people might be doubtful about the sincerity of such supporters. They would prefer to keep the movement pure and far away from anything that smells of the military. I think this would be a mistake. The road to a peaceful international community is still long and difficult and we need all the help we can get.

NOTES

(The publications mentioned in the footnotes, are described more fully in the list of literature.)

1. The contribution to this book by Anders Boserup deals more fully with the connection between disarmament and alternative defence strategies.
2. For instance Roberts (1969), Ebert and Boserup/Mack. These books contain further references.
3. Roberts, 'Civilian Defence Twenty Years On', in *Bulletin of Peace Proposals,* 1978:4.
4. Roberts, 1976, page 34.
5. There is an interesting parallel here with discussions about the limits of large scale industrial enterprise and the possibilities of using micro-electronics to decentralise the economy.
6. Afheldt, 1976.
7. For instance Burt, Digby, Kemp. A recent extensive survey of the field can be found in the articles by Hewish.
8. The Adelphi Paper by Stephen Canby is an early example, which attracted a lot of attention at the time.
9. Spannocchi and Brossolet, 1976, p. 39.
10. Idem., p. 49.
11. Udo Philipp in *Internationale Wehrrevue.*
12. Löser, 1980, p. 121.
13. A corresponding view, emphasising well prepared defensive positions, can be found in the article by Tillson.
14. Uhle-Wettler, 1980, p. 8.
15. Spinney, 1980, p. 30.
16. Since Spinney's presentation became known, this theme has been picked up by several others in the press; see Fallows, *Newsweek.*
17. Spinney, p. 38.
18. For the position of the electronics industry in relation to other branches of industry, see also Kaldor's recent book.

BIBLIOGRAPHY

1. Horst Afheldt, *Verteidigung und Frieden,* Hanser Verlag, Munich, 1976.
2. A. Arnhard, "Zum konventionellen Kriegsbild", in *Europäische Wehrkunde,* 1981, nr. 6.
3. 'Alternative Sicherheitskonzepte', in *Antimilitarismus Information, 1981: 3.*
4. *Bulletin of Peace Proposals, 1978:4* (Alternative Defence and Security).
5. Anders Boserup, Andrew Mack, *War Without Weapons,* (Frances Pinter, London, 1974).
6. Richard Burt, 'New Weapons Technologies, Debate and Directions', *Adelphi Paper no. 126,* summer 1978.
7. Steven Canby, 'The Alliance and Europe, Part IV: Military Doctrine and Technology', *Adelphi Paper no. 109,* winter 1974/5.
8. 'Territorial Defence in Central Europe', in *Armed Forces and Society,* Vol. 7, no. 1, Fall 1980.
9. Martin van Creveld, 'Military Lessons of the Yom Kippur War: Historical Perspectives', *The Washington Papers,* vol. III, no. 24.
10. James Digby, 'Precision Guided Weapons', *Adelphi Paper no. 118,* summer 1975.
11. Theodor Ebert, *Gewaltfreier Aufstand, Alternative zum Bürgerkrieg,* Fischer Verlag, 1970.
12. J. Fallows, 'The Great Defense Deception', in *The New York Review of Books,* May 28, 1981.
13. M. Hewish, 'Tactical-missile survey', in *International Defense Review,* 1980: 6. 9: 1981:3.
14. Mary Kaldor, *The Baroque Arsenal* (Andre Deutsch, London, 1982).
15. G. Kemp and others (ed.), *The Other Arms Race,* Lexington Books, Lexington, Mass., 1975.
16. Hans-Joachim Löser, 'Raumdeckende Verteidigung" in *Osterreichische Militär. Zeitschrift,* Heft 1977:4.
17. 'Raumdeckende Verteidigung' gegen 'Raumgreifende Operationen' in *Europäische Wehrkunde,* 1977:9.
18. 'Vorneverteidigung der Bundesrepublik Deutschland?' in *Osterreichische Militär. Zeitschrift,* Heft 1980:2.
19. J.J. Mearsheimer, 'Precision-guided Munitions and Conventional Deterrence', in *Survival,* March/April 1979.
20. F.O. Miksche, *Vom Kriegsbild,* Seewald Verlag, Stuttgart, 1976.
21. 'New Conventional Weapons and East-West Security', *Adelphi Papers 144, 145, Spring 1978.*
22. *Newsweek,* June 8, 1981 (Reagan's Defense Buildup).
23. Udo Philipp, Bonn: 'NATO-Strategie in der Diskussion' in *Internationale Wehrrevue,* 1980:9.
24. Adam Roberts, *Civilian Resistance as a National Defence,* Penguin Books, Harmondsworth, 1969.
25. *Nations in Arms, The Theory and Practice of Territorial Defence,* Chatto and Windus, London, 1976.
26. Emil Spannocchi, Guy Brossolet, *Verteidigung ohne Schlacht,* Hanser Verlag, Munich, 1976.
27. Franklin C. Spinney, *Defense Facts of Life,* Informal Hearing: Senator Nunn's Office, December 5, 1980 (mimeo).
28. J.C.F. Tillson IV, 'The Forward Defence of Europe', in *Military Review,* May 1981.
29. Franz Uhle-Wettler, *Gefechtsfeld Mitteleuropa,* Bernard & Graefe, Munich 1980.

NUCLEAR DISARMAMENT: NON-NUCLEAR DEFENCE

Anders Boserup

What can be done to diminish the nuclear threat in Europe? There is a well-known answer to this question: we must raise the nuclear threshold by achieving a better balance of conventional forces. Since we seem unable to agree with the countries of the Warsaw Pact on appropriate ceilings on conventional forces in Europe, we must instead increase our own conventional forces until we are able to meet any likely threat without having to resort to nuclear weapons. Once we have reached a force level which we deem adequate we can be sure that the other side will find it excessive, and the whole cycle can begin all over again.

What is wrong in this process is very plain. While it is perfectly sensible for us to increase our defensive forces to a point where they match the offensive capability of the other side, the problem is that these defensive forces add to our offensive capability and thereby fuel a further round in the arms race.

Let us then assume for a moment that it is possible to separate weapons and forces into two types: those with an offensive capability and those which can only be used defensively. If this were possible we would soon discover that if we have enough of the latter we would have no need at all for the former, for the only possible use of the offensive-capable forces is as an adjunct to the defence. In the situation in which we find ourselves in Europe as the central area of confrontation for the superpowers it is evident that we cannot afford to have any positive war aims. Whether we like it or not, should war occur, the most we can aim for is the restoration of the *status quo ante*.

We can go one step further: if our defensive forces are

185

sufficient to meet any contingency, if therefore we have no need for and do not possess (or not in great numbers) forces capable of an offensive role then the forces needed on the other side (in so far as they are destined for the European theatre) would be correspondingly less. Were their number diminished our defensive forces could also be diminished.

What we see here is a process of disarmament entirely different from those which we have been discussing for years. It is not unilateral disarmament in the old sense, which is essentially a gamble on the intentions of the opponent or on his willingness to follow suit. Nor is it multilateral (or bilateral) disarmament as ordinarily conceived and practised: endless negotiations which achieve much too little much too late or nothing at all. Instead, it is a set of unilateral steps, each of which is justified by national self-interest alone and does not require reciprocation, but each of which prompts reciprocation (if we may assume that there is on all sides a readiness to cut away sheer waste).

All of this is simply meant to bring out certain fundamental points of an essentially logical nature. I am perfectly aware, of course, of the objection which is normally raised against this line of thought, namely that one cannot make a distinction between offensive and defensive weapons. That is certainly true, if only because any addition to the defence might release other means which can be used offensively. There is no weapon of which it can be said that whatever the circumstances it can only add to the defensive, never to the offensive strength of a country. This is true, but it is not a relevant objection, for while no weapon, weapon system or force component can be said to be, as such, in the abstract, purely defensive, it is perfectly possible for the complete military set-up of a country to be strictly defensive with no offensive capability at all or with only a very limited offensive capability. A defence without long distance transport and with weapons of no very great range would be a case in point. After all, governments do not find it difficult to identify those force components on the other side which threaten stability and justify counter-armament. So there is great scope for governments to consider each other's apprehension and move towards essentially defensive forces.

The distinction between offensive and defensive capability is an absolutely crucial one but it is in such disrepute today that it is almost always ignored. It is a widely held belief, for example, that peace and stability are promoted by a so-called balance of force. Yet it is patently wrong. Even if it could be defined, agreed upon and implemented—which it cannot—an equality of forces does not in the slightest degree guarantee peace and stability. These do not arise, they never have arisen and they never will arise from any kind of equality; they depend upon an *in*equality, namely the superiority of the defensive capabilities over the offensive capabilities of the countries or alliances concerned.

I know very well that a great imbalance of forces—but it has to be very considerable—can be a source of instability and an invitation to war. I have no quarrel with that argument. But it does not follow that a balance of forces ensures or even promotes stability. It does not follow in logic and it does not follow in practice. Yet we seem to be completely trapped by that conception and for years we have been basing all our policies on it.

You can have a balance in quantitative terms which is extremely unstable in crisis and in war. That will be the case when both sides have offensive capabilities well in excess of the defensive capability of the other side. This produces a trigger-happy and escalation-prone situation. You can also have a quantitative balance which gives rise to great stability, to a situation where crises are unlikely to lead to war and where confined acts of warfare, should they occur, are unlikely to lead to much escalation. That will be the case if defensive capabilities on both sides substantially exceed offensive capabilities. Stability in one case and instability in the other have nothing whatsoever to do with the question of balance. It depends solely on the relative strengths of offence and defence. As long as we ignore or deny the validity of this distinction, the defence policies we adopt are bound to lead to muddled confusion at best, disaster at worst.

Relying on nuclear deterrence does not make it safe to suppress this distinction. In deterrence, each side is compelled to sustain and create sources of instability. In a policy based on balancing forces, each threatens the other by over-insuring on the basis of a worst-case analysis, thus engendering the arms race. In recent years many writers have tried to defend deterrence against the emergence of nuclear war-fighting doctrines. These are indeed ghastly and should be opposed. But deterrence is no escape from doctrines and preparations for war-fighting: they too are meant to deter; they are the logical outcome of attempts to preserve the 'credibility' of deterrence in cases where it might be in doubt.

The basic problem in all nuclear deterrence is its inherent lack of credibility. The reprisals envisaged by the strategy are, by definition, wholly disproportionate in their effects and militarily pointless. While one can hope to deter hostile actions by threatening to massacre millions of innocent people, it makes no sense whatever to carry out the threat when the time comes, not even if it can be done with im-punity. For deterrence to be credible, not rational political judgement but insane vindictiveness or some unthinking 'doomsday' device must be seen to be in control. This is not meant to deny that deterrence can work, only to draw attention to its darker side, to the requirements which must be met if it is to be more than a paper tiger. What some writers characterise as the 'excesses' of nuclear deterrence are in fact its requirements: hostility and paranoia, recurrent sabre-rattling, military and political dispositions which pro-mote instability and encourage escalation and a continuing arms race.

The deliberate creation of credible avenues of escalation is the *sine qua non* of deterrence. Deterrence must be genuine-ly dangerous if it is to exist.

It follows that, as Allan Krass and Dan Smith argue in their contribution to this book, there can be no such thing as a 'stable', 'pure' or 'minimal' deterrent. Either it would not deter or it would not remain stable, pure or minimal for long. In fact, stability in deterrence is a self-contradictory notion: it is not possible to have both at once. Nor is it obvious that a minimum deterrent would promote peace and security in the world. Returning to concepts akin to the doctrine of massive retaliation of the 1950s is more likely to promote confrontation, brinkmanship and insecurity, because

188

credibility in real situations would be low. If there were a return to minimum deterrence, sensible people would soon be calling for more 'flexible' and 'graduated' capabilities to achieve deterrence without constantly courting disaster. And so we would quickly move back again into our present mess.

Attempts to salvage deterrence by dissociating 'good' and 'desirable' elements from 'abuses' are futile and will only entangle us in self-contradiction and self-deception. A viable approach to peace, security and disarmament can only be found by seeking a sensible defence policy. Genuine security and arms restraint can only be based on the notion of preserving peace by means of forces which are ample for defence but with offensive capabilities deliberately reduced to a minimum. Only in this way can one state reconcile its demand for security with other states' rights to it.

The question, then, is what can be done to diminish the risk of nuclear war in Europe? The answer is quite straightforward. We must deploy forces which are strong enough in the defensive to meet any contingency without resort to nuclear weapons, and which are *deliberately* weak in the offensive mode. If both East and West do this, only modest forces will be required; if Western countries do it unilaterally, very substantial forces will be needed.

Furthermore these forces must be arranged so that they do not provide meaningful military targets for the nuclear weapons of the enemy. For this reason they must be widely dispersed and mobile, and able to function independently of any logistic installations, airfields, harbours and the like.

If we can meet these requirements then, should war occur, we on our side shall not *need* to use nuclear weapons for military purposes and the enemy will not be *able* to do so.

I do not deny that the enemy would still have the option of striking at civilian targets. It is always 'conceivable'—but 'conceivable' is a very weak term—that an enemy would bomb our cities to break our will to resist. As long as nuclear weapons exist there can be no final, absolute guarantees against such a possibility. But if our forces pose no threat to the enemy, and if the possibility remains—as it would in any case—that the United States might strike back, then the idea

189

that an enemy who cannot cope with our military forces in the field would try to conquer us by bombing us into submission seems to be decidedly far-fetched. Nuclear war through sheer madness or vindictiveness remains a possibility, but the real problem that we are facing is not that of irrational acts which are just barely conceivable, but that of acts which do seem rational to the enemy in a certain political and strategic context.

It must be stressed that a defence meeting the above requirements is capable of dealing effectively with the nuclear threat only because, and only in so far as it is based on a strictly defensive force deployment. If it is only our *intentions* which are defensive, if we do not take the full step of emasculating the offensive capability of our own forces, if we fail to recognise that in a nuclear environment it is in our own best interest to ensure that our potential enemies do not fear us, then nothing is achieved, and we are back in the present predicament of mutual fears and an unbridled arms race. However much we may have managed to diminish the vulnerability of our military forces to nuclear attack, the overall nuclear threat will remain.

Whatever we do in Europe, warfare in our continent will take place in the shadow of the bipolar nuclear confrontation of the superpowers. This fact imposes upon us the absence of positive war aims and forces us to aim for nothing better in war than the restoration of the *status quo ante*. In turn, it is this limitation of the aims which makes it politically possible to have a strategy based on a pure defensive, since such a strategy involves no sacrifice beyond that which we have to make in any case. It is therefore the objective conditions of warfare in our continent which create the conditions of existence for such a strategy. That is why it cannot be regarded as just a general means of coping with any conventional threat but is specifically a strategy for promoting peace and security in the kind of nuclear environment which we have in Europe.

Is it also possible to implement such a strategy in practice? In other words, is it possible to design conventional forces which have the required characteristics? Is it technically and economically feasible? This is not a question which can be answered generally with a 'yes' or 'no'. One would have to consider each region of Europe separately and design the specific forces to be used in each case in the light of the military geography and the specific strategic role of each region. Clearly, the precise solutions called for are quite different in the plains of Northern Germany, in the Danish archipelago and in the fjords of Norway.

Without going into the details of what such forces might look like in each specfic situation, it can be noted that present developments in military technology are increasingly making possible forces of precisely the kind required. The classical weapon platforms of the industrial age—aircraft, ships and armoured vehicles—which any attacker must use in bulk, are becoming highly vulnerable to, or, if you like, too expensive to protect against the precision-guided munitions which are being developed. Small groups of men armed with such weapons can have an enormous firepower. Thus it is becoming possible to design forces composed of small units, widely dispersed and difficult to seek and destroy. These would be forces which do not themselves make use of the classical weapon platforms, which are therefore not vulnerable to the types of weapons which they themselves possess, and whose offensive capability would be extremely low, but which have a great capability for defence against an intruding force, whether over land, by sea or by air.

I am sure that one can find areas for which it would be difficult to design strictly defensive, invulnerable forces of the type discussed here and which would on their own have a sufficient defensive capability to meet all the worst contingencies which can be dreamt up. But this does not invalidate the approach. Even if we find that we cannot replace all the forces in western Europe by such defensive forces, partial steps in this direction would still go a long way towards increasing security and stability in this continent. This also means that a gradual approach is possible, and for that reason my chief purpose here has been to indicate the general direction in which we should move. If we are seriously concerned to abolish the nuclear threat in Europe, we have to begin to determine the kinds of solutions which would be applicable in each area. Ben

Dankbaar's chapter in this book surveys the work which has already been done on this kind of approach. This work needs to be taken further and discussed more widely. No task is more urgent than proceeding with the development of credible alternative military defence systems which can render our nuclear forces unnecessary and those of potential enemies unuseable.

In three decades of the arms race we have managed, in terms of security in Europe, to get ourselves into the most frightful mess. I have tried to show that the situation, nevertheless, is not beyond repair, but for improvement to be possible it is necessary that we recognise that the situation of Europe as a heavily armed main area of confrontation between the nuclear superpowers demands a completely different approach to deterrence, i.e. to war prevention, than the approach which brought us where we are. Deterrence through balance of *power* made some sense in pre-nuclear Europe. Deterrence through balance of *terror* and the logic of escalation can appear to make some slight sense for the nuclear powers themselves in the neat and orderly world of the textbooks. In the European mess we need something different: different from the balance of power, different from the balance of terror, and different, certainly, from the confused and self-contradictory mixture of both which, today, passes for the ultimate in strategic subtlety. I have tried to indicate that once we rid ourselves of mere prejudice and base ourselves on a clear understanding of the global situation which determines the strategic conditions in Europe it is not so difficult to see the principles on which real security can be built.

GLOSSARY

ABM	Anti-Ballistic Missile
ADM	Atomic Demolition Munitions
AFL-CIO	American Federation of Labour and Congress of Industrial Organizations
ANZUS	Australia, New Zealand and the United States, an area alliance
ASALM	Advanced Strategic Air-Launched Missile
ASAT	Anti-Satellite Warfare
ASW	Anti-Submarine Warfare
BVR	Beyond Visual Range
CEP	Circular Error Probable
CENTO	Central Treaty Organisation, a former US treaty organisation in the Middle East
C^3I	Command, Control, Communications and Intelligence
CIA	Central Intelligence Agency
CND	Campaign for Nuclear Disarmament
END	European Nuclear Disarmament
FBS	Forward Based Systems
FROG	Free Rocket Over Ground
GLCM	Ground-Launched Cruise Missile
ICBM	Intercontinental Ballistic Missile
IISS	International Institute of Strategic Studies
IRBM	Intermediate-Range Ballistic Missile
LRCM	Long-Range Cruise Missile
LRTNF	Long-Range Theatre Nuclear Forces
MBFR	Mutual and Balanced Force Reductions
MIRV	Multiple Independently-Targeted Re-entry Vehicles
MLF	Multilateral Force

193

MRBM	Medium-Range Ballistic Missile
NATO	North Atlantic Treaty Organisation
NFZ, NWFZ	Nuclear-Free Zone, Nuclear-Weapon-Free Zone
PCI	Italian Communist Party
PGM	Precision Guided Munitions
RADAG	Radar Terminal Guidance
SACEUR	Supreme Allied Commander Europe
SALT	Strategic Arms Limitation Talks
SEATO	South-East Asia Treaty Organisation
SHAPE	NATO Headquarters
SLBM	Submarine-Launched Ballistic Missile
SPD	West German Social Democratic Party
TNF	Theatre Nuclear Forces
TNT	Trinitre-toluene, a conventional explosive
TNW	Theatre Nuclear Weapons
UN	United Nations

NOTES ON AUTHORS

Ulrich Albrecht is a Vice President and Professor of peace research at the Free University of Berlin. He is the author of many books and articles on arms production and the arms trade.

Erik Alfsen is Professor of Mathematics at the University of Oslo and an organiser of NEJ TIL ATOMVAPEN in Norway.

William Arkin formerly worked for American Army intelligence and the Centre for Defense Information in Washington. He is now a Fellow of the Institute for policy studies in Washington and the author of *Research Guide to Current Military and Strategic Affairs.*

Anders Boserup is Professor of Sociology at the University of Copenhagen. He is Co-Chairman of the Danish Royal Commission on Defence and Disarmament and has acted as consultant for the United Nations on various disarmament issues.

Ben Dankbaar teaches Economics in the University of Amsterdam and also writes articles about military affairs for a Dutch journal. He has been very much involved in the Dutch armed forces movement.

David Holloway is a lecturer in politics at the University of Edinburgh currently working on the Peace Studies programme at Cornell University. He is the author of many works on military technology in the Soviet Union.

Mary Kaldor is a Fellow of the Science Policy Research Unit and the Institute for Development Studies at Sussex University. She is the author of *The Disintegrating West* (1978) and *The Baroque Arsenal* (1982). She is on the END Coordinating Committee.

István Kende is Professor Emeritus of International Relations at the University of Budapest. He is an active member of PUGWASH and the author of books and articles about conflict in the modern world.

Allan Krass is Professor of Physics and Science at Hampshire College in Massachussetts. As a Visiting Researcher at the Stockholm International Peace Research Institute in 1980/1 he wrote a chapter for the

SIPRI Yearbook 1981 entitled 'The Evolution of Military Technology and Deterrence Strategy' and co-authored *The Enrichment Route to Proliferation.*

Sverre Lodgaard is a researcher at the Peace Research Institute Oslo and he is currently spending some time at the Stockholm International Peace Research Institute to work on European security problems.

Dan Smith is author of *The Defence of the Realm in the 1980s* (1980) and co-editor of *Protest and Survive* (1980). He is a member of the CND National Council and END Coordinating Committee.